9.75

Essay In  P9-AGA-196

2-10-72

A BOOK FOR BOOKMEN

A BOOK FOR BOOKMEN

Being

Edited Manuscripts & Marginalia

With

Essays on Several Occasions

By

JOHN DRINKWATER

Essay Index Reprint Series

Essay Index

BOOKS FOR LIBRARIES PRESS
FREEPORT, NEW YORK

First Published 1927
Reprinted 1968

LIBRARY OF CONGRESS CATALOG CARD NUMBER:

68-29201

PRINTED IN THE UNITED STATES OF AMERICA

PREFACE

THIS is designed to be a book for bookmen; my hope is that it may provide some entertainment for serendipity minds at the half-hour before the light is switched off or blown out at night.

I have here edited some of the letters, marginal notes, and less important scraps that I have collected over a number of years. They range from the valuable notes of Coleridge on Warton's Milton down to such *trivia* as Rogers's proposal of Prosper Mérimée for the Athenæum. Where I have printed from MS. my assumption is that this is the first appearance of the material in print, which may some day help to tease the bibliographers. I have included a few brief essays on purely bookish matters without MS. material, and a few on authors who may look for attention rather from the curious than the general reader.

I have to thank Mr. Clement K. Shorter, the Rev. G. H. G. Coleridge, Lady Sandhurst and Messrs. Macmillan and Co., Ltd., and Miss Evelyn Darley for courtesies as to copyright, and the editors of *The Cornhill Magazine*, *The Fortnightly Review*, *The London Mercury*, and *The Sunday Times* for their hospitality. The paper on William Cory appeared in the fourth volume of *Essays by Divers Hands,* and that on Branwell Brontë was privately printed (1924) in an edition of his Horace translations, to which some readers of the essay may wish to refer. The Hartley Coleridge, Hawker and Barnes papers were written for selections from their works published by Mr. Blackwell; in each case the second section is an addition.

J. D.

London.
May, 1926.

CONTENTS

PAGE

WILLIAM CORY 1

PATRICK BRANWELL BRONTË 41

COLERIDGE, MILTON, AND WARTON . . . 61

COLERIDGE'S *ZAPOLYA* 93

LANDOR'S *DRY STICKS FAGOTED* . . . 101

JOHN COLLOP 115

A POEM BY CHRISTOPHER SMART . . . 135

ERASMUS DARWIN 141

HARTLEY COLERIDGE 155

ROBERT STEPHEN HAWKER 167

WILLIAM BARNES 179

MR. WISE'S "ASHLEY CATALOGUE" . . . 189

THE LIBRARY OF A MAN OF LETTERS . . 197

A MEMORY OF GEORGE D. SMITH . . . 205

SOME LETTERS FROM MATTHEW ARNOLD TO
ROBERT BROWNING 213

SOME UNPUBLISHED LETTERS 233

    WILLIAM SHENSTONE 235

    JAMES BEATTIE 242

    GEORGE CRABBE 245

    SAMUEL ROGERS 252

    SAMUEL TAYLOR COLERIDGE . . . 253

    ROBERT BLOOMFIELD 257

    JOHN CLARE 264

    GEORGE DARLEY 268

    ALLAN CUNNINGHAM 279

WILLIAM CORY

WILLIAM CORY

I.

WILLIAM CORY—he was William Johnson by birth and took the name of Cory in 1872 for family reasons—was born in January, 1823, and died in 1892, a few months before reaching the age of seventy. Cory was a poet, of slight and desultory genius, writing and publishing very little verse, and yet with a secure though slender claim to " a permanent place," as the *Dictionary of National Biography* puts it, " among English lyrists." He is in that work wrongly credited with several volumes of poems. In fact he published, apart from a few classical experiments composed chiefly in the nature of school exercises, but two small pamphlets of verse. The first of these, *Ionica*,* appeared in 1858, from the house of Smith Elder, and it was followed in 1877 by the privately printed *Ionica* II., containing a further twenty-five poems. Both of these little volumes appeared anonymously. In 1891 he added a few new poems to the old ones, and published them together, retaining the original title, with George Allen, the authorship still being unacknowledged.

* *Ionica* had been preceded in 1843 by the prize poem *Plato*, which obtained the Chancellor's medal at Cambridge in that year.

Small as the volume of Cory's poems is, it is yet considerably smaller when it is reduced to those pieces by which his reputation as a lyrist is established. For the most part the verses are marked more clearly by personality than by lyric success. Cory himself was always shy about their publication, considering them to be rather the occasional notes of personal intimacies and circumstance, not designed for a wider public. Having been a boy at Eton himself, he left Cambridge after a brilliant career to take up a mastership in that school, and he remained there for twenty-seven years. Of the devotion and the beauty of character which he brought to his task, and kept unspoilt through the long term of its exercise, more is to be said, but it may here be noted that many of his verses are the charming, but slight and closely personal, record of the contacts and occasions of those years. His poetic gift, however, could be used to much more general effect, and lying among the more occasional pages of his book are to be found others that will continue to delight the readers that they may find. *Mimnermus in Church*, *Amaturus*, *A Queen's Visit*, *After reading " Maud,"* *A Cruise*, *A Fable*, *A Ballad for a Boy*, *Barine*, *Mir ist Leide*, *Remember*, *An Apology*, *Reparabo*, *Prospero*, and *Heraclitus*, seem to me to be the pick of these, and they make a little sheaf fine enough in quality to keep Cory's name fresh in English poetry. Here are two of them:

Reparabo.

The world will rob me of my friends,
  For time with her conspires;
But they shall both to make amends
  Relight my slumbering fires.

For while my comrades pass away
  To bow and smirk and gloze,
Come others, for as short a stay;
  And dear are these as those.

And who was this? they ask; and then
  The loved and lost I praise:
" Like you they frolicked; they are men;
  Bless ye my later days."

Why fret? the hawks I trained are flown:
  'Twas nature bade them range;
I could not keep their wings half-grown,
  I could not bar the change.

With lattice opened wide I stand
  To watch their eager flight;
With broken jesses in my hand
  I muse on their delight.

And, oh! if one with sullied plume
  Should droop in mid career,
My love makes signals:—" There is room,
  Oh bleeding wanderer, here. "

Heraclitus.

They told me, Heraclitus, they told me you were dead,
They brought me bitter news to hear and bitter tears to shed
I wept as I remember'd how often you and I
Had tired the sun with talking and sent him down the sky.

And now that thou art lying, my dear old Carian guest,
A handful of grey ashes, long, long ago at rest,
Still are thy pleasant voices, thy nightingales, awake;
For death, he taketh all away, but them he cannot take.

Heraclitus is both Cory's best and his most celebrated poem. In its company some of the other pieces will survive, as they should do, but without it they would probably fall into neglect. In reading the lovely lines—

I wept as I remember'd how often you and I
Had tired the sun with talking and sent him down the sky . . .

it is interesting to recall a passage in Lord Lyttelton's Elegy on his wife published in 1747:

In vain I look around
O'er all the well-known Ground
My Lucy's wonted Footsteps to descry:
Where oft we us'd to walk,
Where oft in tender Talk
We saw the Summer Sun go down the Sky.

Heraclitus, translation or rendering though it is, becomes a perfect English lyric, and while some of Cory's other poems are worthy of a place beside it, none can be said quite to match it.

II.

While, however, the claims of Cory's verse may, in their own modest though distinguished way, be readily allowed, he gave little of his time or energy to poetical composition, and it was not as a poet that he most readily expressed himself. He belonged to a type that we are tempted to consider as being peculiarly English. A liberal classical education and a fine general culture combined in him to produce a mind observant, inquisitive, and lucidly critical. This is admirable enough, but not uncommon. The uncommon thing is when such a mind, constantly exercised as it is apt to be in a wide range of insistent but ephemeral interests, retains a genuinely unsophisticated delight in profound emotional simplicities; when, in other words, the poetry of a mind is not destroyed by the constant application of affairs, by keeping abreast of current events. And this happy constitution of mind, though it must always be rare, is, it might seem, commoner in Englishmen than in most. What is meant is something far more than the mere educated interest in art and letters which may be found often enough in men of affairs the world over. It is the gift of submitting all events and institutions, as they have to be dealt with, not only to history, but to the imaginative wisdom which is the flower of the universal mind—in fact to poetry. It is, further, a gift that moves beyond a sense of this admirable necessity into the regions of independent

creation.   Our literature is rich in the names of men
who have achieved great distinction as writers, without
having ·been devoted wholly to the calling of letters.
Spenser, Sidney, Bacon, Marvell—the succession could
be shown down to men like Lord Morley and Lord
Rosebery and Sir Ronald Ross in our own time.
It is true that the achievement of such writers is
generally rather in the fields of critical or philosophical
than of imaginative literature, though there are
obvious exceptions.   The reason is plain.   Men of
affairs, whether in commerce or the professions or
politics, when the demands of their calling are satisfied, can very rarely be expected to have a surplus
energy equal to imaginative creation.   The surprising
thing is that so many of them have, if not this energy,
at least a reserve of power left that enables them to
contribute seriously, by the best standards, to literature
of a high, if not often of the highest order.

William Cory, in the natural movements of his
mind, was a great man of affairs.   This claim may
seem to be extravagant, and remembering the seclusion
of his Eton mastership, to be followed by a yet greater
seclusion, when at the age of forty-seven he became
a country squire, never again to take up any more active
occupation, it is clear that I do not mean a great man
of affairs in the ordinary sense.   I said in the natural
movements of his mind.   By circumstance Cory was
a diligent schoolmaster, a lonely and fastidious scholar,
a gentle and very occasional poet.   But by instinct he
belonged to, and by his interests he lived in, the great

world of affairs, the world of statesmanship and political crises, of wars and social reforms, of national designs and industry, with an intense and persistent ardour. Though he was not a man of action, either under arms or in office, he spent as much energy as though he had been closely engaged himself. Almost his only literary production, apart from his poems, and a long series of letters, written for the most part to men who had been under him at Eton, was a journal which he kept, and of which he says himself, " I do every vacation write a genuine original book, my journal for about three readers. . . . I believe every man of sensibility might with some advantage do this, omitting all megrims, grumblings and sneers." This journal, with a considerable selection of the letters, was privately published in 1897 for something over twenty subscribers. How many copies of the book were printed I do not know, but it has become a rare volume. A popular edition is, I believe, now in contemplation. Both journal and letters, which together run to nearly six hundred pages and make very attractive reading throughout, are packed with observation and criticism of the dominant personalities and events of the Victorian stage. Literature is a constant subject of his reflection, but he confines himself usually in this matter to summary judgments, while his commentary upon current politics in all their ramifications is minutely argued and widely informed. And in this fact lies the explanation, perhaps, of Cory's meagre productivity as a poet. He was in his journal and letters (he probably was also in his personal relations) an immense talker, and while he was a match for anyone in scholarship, and historical perspective, and literary knowledge, when these were needed, he yet more freely talked of the great network of current politics and affairs with exhaustive information on his subject. And such talk inevitably dissipates the concentration necessary to sustained poetic production. In his later years he speaks of the renewed delight, when an occasional visitor of intellectual parts went to see him in his Devonshire seclusion, of improvising original opinions in conversation. The delight is one in which we all at times fondly imagine we share, but the creative mind indulges it with any freedom only at great risk, while to the true talker it becomes an almost daily necessity. And Cory was a true talker. The improvisation of which he speaks was never irresponsible or unrelated to conviction or standards, but it was improvisation in the special sense that creation is not. His aims were not brilliance or dialectic victory; indeed, he tells us at the age of twenty-four that the true purpose of discussion is to make " a minute comparison of minds without argument," and again twenty years later, that the use of Cambridge debates was " to lay minds fairly alongside of each other." But none the less this preoccupation of his with affairs did lead him constantly, as it always does, into attaching undue importance to the things of sound and fury that in the long run signify but little more than nothing. His journal pages are full of earnest and even heated arguments that have long since been swept away in the litter of forgotten controversy, and are now only redeemed from mere dulness by the faintly surviving charm of Cory's presentation. These parts of the journal show us a man touched by that garrulousness of intellect which, even though it be truly of intellect, forbids the deeper and simpler contemplations of poetry, and we have to return to other parts of the journal and to *Ionica* to be reminded that Cory was a poet at all.

III.

And of Cory's essential poetic character there is in these other parts of the journal abundant evidence to place beside *Ionica*. In his vacations and in the freedom of his later years he travelled a good deal, and the accounts in his journal of the places that he visits are vivid with observation and allusion. Association was inevitably precious to a mind so richly stored. "What travelling," he asked, "is like that which takes one to the haunts of poets and the sanctuaries of historical nations." The common heritage of poets, a sense of beauty's transience, is strong in him. In Westminster Abbey, he tells us that he is far more moved by the epitaphs than by the sermons, "implicitly believing that the irrecoverable souls were as fair as the marbles say they were, longing to know them, pitying them for being dead, pitying their kinsfolk who lost them so long ago." When he is abroad, however, it is not so much in the brilliant descriptive strokes that enliven his journal that we find the essentially poetic character asserting itself, as in a passion that unifies the experiences of his travel. In Cory's case the passion was patriotism, " the sweep and splendour of England's war," as Sir Henry Newbolt puts it in his fine elegy, the war being one that transcends the local habitation of the battlefield. In almost everything he saw abroad, of peoples and customs and institutions, he found some reflection of England's honour or failure, and his jealousy that she should nobly fulfil what he conceived to be her mission in the world was constant. Whether or not his political ambitions for his country made for general human good to the degree that he believed we need not discuss here, but that they burned in his spirit with an absolute purity there can be no doubt. The only misgiving—almost certainly an unjust and ungenerous one—we ever have in the presence of his passionate loyalty is when he, from his gentle seclusion, urges others to fierce and dangerous action. Given the circumstances, Cory would, we are sure, without hesitation have died for his country himself, but the misgiving persists because the answer is not quite complete. However this may be, in hardly any other way do we ever question the character that presents itself in the journal and letters.

Lord Esher, in his newly published volume, *Ionicus*, is right in attributing Mr. A. C. Benson's assertion that Cory's was " probably one of the most vigorous and commanding minds of the century " to friendly exaggeration, but there can be no doubt that it would be difficult to exaggerate the influence that he had upon his pupils, both at Eton and in their later life. And these pupils included a large group of men who came to the highest distinction in the public life of their time. The *Letters and Journals* are full of communication with or reference to Lord Rosebery, Lord Balfour, Alfred Lyttelton, and a score of other men whose names are less remembered now, but who were of equal eminence in their day. With many of these he kept in constant touch till the end of his life, as Lord Esher's volume, containing as he says only a quarter of the letters Cory wrote to him, shows, and Lord Esher's devotion to his old master is clearly characteristic of many such life-long loyalties in other pupils. With many of his Eton boys Cory corresponded before the end of their schooldays, when they were away on vacation or sick-leave, and he had the great gift of talking to them already without the slightest intellectual condescension. Nothing could be more charming than the unaffected gravity with which he can ask a boy of fifteen for his advice and opinion.*

* In 1898 the Oxford Press published a pamphlet, *Hints for Eton Masters*, by W. J——, taken from a manuscript journal of 1862. It is full of wise counsel to pedagogues, and a charming product of Cory's lively style. The following note upon not giving sufficient credit for work well done in school is characteristic: " If we cheered those who play our bowling in school well, as heartily as we cheer our batsmen at Lord's, I think there would be a little more zeal amongst our young students."

Although he was a brave and far from unhappy man, Cory after the first brilliant promise of his Cambridge days always carried with him something of a sense of failure. He was never robust, and he was so near-sighted as to be almost blind at any distance, until he delightedly discovered the use of a spy-glass. He was very well aware, too, of the constraint upon achievement that the routine of Eton meant. He did not complain, he was, indeed, on the whole satisfied that the ways of his life were happily chosen, but we feel all the time that he would have liked to have some wider administrative power, that he would have liked to impress his scholarship more brilliantly upon his age, that he would have liked to accomplish more as a writer, that, above all, he would have liked to set his name among the heroes that he worshipped. "The cavalry weapon against unbroken infantry is the horse. Let one man make a hole, live or die in it, the square is pierced. The Germans did it at Salamanca. I would like to end my life that way, if the square were made of Russian diplomats, motherless, wifeless, and sisterless." So he wrote when he was over fifty, in the spirit in which as a young master at Eton he had taken the boys out of the classroom to see the Guards marching down the street, with the admonition, "Brats, the British army!" But he was early aware of the narrowness of his destiny, sometimes poignantly, sometimes humorously. When he was twenty-five the modern history professorship at Cambridge fell vacant, and his name seems to have been mentioned. He notes, " I should never be man enough for a place like Cambridge, but at a second-rate university I should make a good history professor as things go." At forty he recalls the eager ambitions of early days, when he little thought that after all he " was to be nothing but a third-rate grammar-monger." And a year or two later there is this entry in the journal: " There are many days, weeks, months, in which I feel like a fungus in a retired part of a kitchen garden —forgotten, left out, useless. Then comes a torrent of notices more or less indicative of regard or consideration, and I am lifted into the honours of a conspicuous dandelion. . . . At luncheon appeared my pupil with a note from his mother asking me to dinner, so that the dandelion became a dahlia."

By the time he was forty he seems to have put ambition by. He notes his departure from a country house thus: " Lady M. gave me a fragrant geranium leaf at parting, and the boy saw me off; and in two hours I had relapsed into my average dulness." About the same time he remarks, " A family that knows illness has the due chiaroscuro," but for himself he has found " something that looks very like health . . . and I have sometimes been very nearly free from self-pity." Self-pity, indeed, was not one of his indulgences. At the age of fifty, on returning from Eton, he took over Halsdon, the small family estate in Devonshire, of which he had acquired a lease. " I am not well; and half my time I meditate the ceremony of dying, but the other half I bud with schemes for the enjoyment of my liberty." But by then his character was mellowed, and his mind, disciplined to its own sphere, " in beautiful order," as he said of one of his own pupils. From his hermitage at Halsdon he can still fret and argue about affairs when he is provoked by some ministerial stupidity, or what he takes to be some heresy in an old pupil, but his daily habit is now one of gentle and often idyllic contemplation, and a lyric delight in the seasons of his little farm and his squirearchic duties. His wish to own twelve cows, expressed many years before at Eton, has come true, and the shrubs and walks are a serious business, with fifty little rhododendrons from Windsor Park—" the Queen's own "—to be planted, and occasional distributions of plants and flowers among gardens less favoured than his own.

And now it is that all the Virgilian sweetness in him asserts itself. There are passages in the journal that have an exquisite satisfaction of phrase, such as when years before he spoke of the codling tarts at his Eton feasts.

He writes in a letter of August, 1874:

" Robert and I last night attacked the hornets who live in the hollow tree on which hangs the gate through which goes Grizzle to fetch grist from Dolton Mill.

" Robert was in the poncho or chasuble and a muslin veil. He directed me; I held a long stick with a brimstone rag. Hornets now and then dropt into burning straw—they were as stupid as the French in Strasbourg, and made no sortie.

" To-night we assist a more nimble sort of enemies, ' apple-drones,' or wasps, close to the stable. R. goes to the town to buy brimstone. I have prepared a sea-kail pot which is to go over the hole, and a dozen dead treelets—' our failures ' (as Beau Brummell said of his cravats). I hope we shall not burn the thatch of the stable. . . .

" There has been a burst of new flowers, not weeds, and birds singing and owls talking to each other since you went."

He talks of the children who are his friends, and says that the " choice thing for girls is to go up the ladders and peep at the pigeons' nests to count the eggs therein." And then again:

" I have four lambs, born in March, quite untameable.

" I have a friend among the percher birds. He comes to breakfast; but he won't let me come near enough to see whether he is a robin or a chaffinch.

" I miss the stable-boy, Jan, who used to show me the nests. . . ."

He has a party in the barn which costs four pounds. " Just compare that with a London or even a Dolton rectory dinner-party, and then compare the aggregate of impressions made at the two; imagine the sweet little thrill it gives a Dolton girl, of the humblest birth, to come down and sing to us *Who is Sylvia?* . . . Whereas when your rich people go to a dinner-party they think no more of it than I do of brushing my hair." He stayed at Halsdon until 1878, when he was fifty-five, receiving old Eton and Cambridge friends as visitors from time to time, faithfully discharging his local responsibilities, and forming very genuine attachments with his farm servants, some of whom he afterwards pensioned with no particular obligation and out of small means. His generosity was always punctilious. Directly he could afford it he gave up his Cambridge fellowship, thinking it improper to be an unnecessary charge on the College funds. Years before, writing to a young correspondent from Eton, after a friendly lecture on University economy, he had concluded: "If you want money to hire a coach, mathematical or otherwise, I beg that you will not take it from the other claims, but let me advance it, and you may repay all such sums, £100 if you like, when you are a prosperous man ten years hence or so." He went from Halsdon to Madeira, where he surprised his friends by marrying. He had one son, Mr. Andrew Cory, who is still alive, to whom as a child the letters contain many touching references. "When I sit, as I do every night on duty, by Andrew's bedside, I am truly content, yet I weep every day to think of having to leave him." That was in 1881. William Cory lived another ten years, coming back to London and dying in Hampstead in 1892. His later years, in spite of precarious health, lost nothing in shrewdness of mind or buoyancy of spirit. His excursions in political criticism and prophecy were as penetrating as ever, and often borne out by the event. "Rule, Britannia" was a favourite tag in his letters. He published the two volumes of *A Guide to Modern English History*

about the time he left Halsdon, and the new edition
of *Ionica* the year before he died. These, apart
from a few occasional papers, make the sum of his
literary production. He read eagerly and widely,
fiction, drama, history, biography, and Lord Esher
tells us of a constant flow of books from house to
house: "If you are in cash I advise you to buy it
before it gets out of print, the Oxford Press, five
volumes, Hill's Boswell, a monumental book. When
I have got through Lecky I am going to read Pollock
on Torts."

IV.

Literature, it goes without saying, was a constant
and presiding interest in Cory's life. He might say:
"Our literature is a supreme blessing to us, yet I
find in my loneliness still more comfort in the sustained action of our nation: Graham at Malaga
shying stones at the assassins, and Baker trampling
on the demons of the Equator, and Glover raising
recruits on the Gold Coast . . . all this is real
meat and drink to me," but his enthusiasm for letters
was more fundamental than this might suggest. The
literary judgments that he gives us are, as I have
said, seldom as closely argued as his political criticism.
They are as often as not merely a statement of likes
and dislikes, but knowing Cory we may find a mere
catalogue of his preferences instructive. His taste
was fine, but often, as it seems to us, strangely cap-
ricious—that is to say, he was never in danger of

liking a bad thing, but he was often iconoclastic and
even merely prejudiced. His prejudices were sometimes coloured by political considerations, which
made him see in Shelley "a Bashi Bazouk and an
enemy of England," or by a certain genteel morality
which led him into the ineffable stupidity of dismissing
Burns as a sot, though he pays tribute to the Scot's
genius elsewhere, and an immense and sometimes
almost overweening faith in his own age, which made
him assert with great conviction that Tennyson was
to be rated far above Milton. Tennyson was indeed
his hero in poetry. "It is now exactly forty years
since Tennyson has been to me the light and charm
of my poor life." And again: "Tennyson is the sum
and product of the art that began with Homer. I
cannot say that he is greater than Homer; but he
fills my soul and makes the best part of forty years of
manhood that I have gone through." Wordsworth
meant much to him, though apparently a good deal
less than Tennyson:

"Mat Arnold's paper in *Macmillan* on *Wordsworth*
hits the nail on the head now and then: he names as his
favourites *Michael, Highland Reaper*, and the *Fountain ;*
he did not seem to see that most of the gems of Wordsworth are rather slight things to build so great a name
upon: a man who tries to make a big thing, and fails
again and again, can hardly be put anywhere near
Milton."

When he is in the Lakes he writes: "Perhaps this
perfect country might have engendered a better poet;

but we owe him (Wordsworth) much," and then in a few weeks he returns to the same subject with: "We are the sons of Wordsworth, and after a quarter of a century which has fed us with highly-spiced dainties, here we are back again with the unlearned prophet of Nature, back to our moonlight and mountain shadows, and the healing touch of Nature." He rather fancied himself as a heretic about Shakespeare. He acknowledged freely the supremacy of Shakespeare's poetry, but he pertinaciously refused to allow an equal supremacy to the dramatist. He saw good plot structure in *The Tempest*, *Othello*, and *Hamlet*, but he thought that the author of these must himself smile at those who called *Lear* a fine play, and that he would have laughed at anyone who thought he meant to stand by such things, among others, as *Twelfth Night* and *Measure for Measure*. Cory's views on drama generally were, indeed, perverted by a partiality for the French theatre that amounted almost to infatuation, and when he was sixty years of age he could say: "I firmly refuse to think Shakespeare a better playwright than Sardou." And his obsession sweeps away the Greeks with Shakespeare—"Greek plays are to French plays what cold boiled veal is to snipe." Even *Othello* he will only allow to be "nearly as good as it was possible for anything to be before the human mind had by evolution become capable of *Kenilworth* and *Maion de Lorme*." He was, indeed, as he claimed, *enfant du siècle*. "It astonishes me that men do not perceive how much greater our age is than other ages."

And as for *Kenilworth*, Scott was perhaps the writer
of all others who enchained his affections most securely
from first to last. " I hold that *Heart of Midlothian*
was very much more effective on the minds of Britons
than all the Lake poets put together. I hold that
Scott is the supreme man of letters after W. S. and
before our lot, Tennyson, G. Eliot, and Currer Bell."

These are opinions not calling for discussion, but,
arbitrary as they are, stamped by personality, and
in themselves suggestive of a figure that was representative of a peculiar aspect of English character.
Still less do we wish to argue with him about his
judgment upon writers who had a far slighter hold
upon his interest either one way or the other. But,
again, some of these casual impressions are worth
noting. As a boy of twenty he rejoiced in Macaulay's
Lays, and at forty, skimming through *Pilgrim's
Progress*, he " thought it wretched stuff and wondered
Macaulay could praise it so highly." He thought
highly of George Eliot, but he did not like Goethe,
and he is betrayed by Matthew Arnold's prose into
the one cruel and bitter remark to be found in his
correspondence. He is often dictatorial and obstinate,
but on this occasion only does he offend against the
ordinary canons of good taste, and the offending
passage ought not to have been written, still less
published.* He honours Spenser as being " in the

* It is fair to say that elsewhere Cory speaks of Arnold with proper
respect. Instances may be found in *Gathered Leaves*, by Mary
Coleridge, 1910, where a chapter on the *Table-Talk of William Cory*

succession," but he cannot read him " except as I can listen to an Archdeacon's sermon. It is a task." He thought Stevenson's *Child's Garden of Verses* was a failure, and that Dickens · had lowered the standard of writing in England, but he could " understand insular people, with no academy to correct their taste, being bewitched by Dickens," while " Thackeray is not even clever, not even strong; it is all of it just the stuff, easy to understand, which one would serve up for the common idler of watering places and parsonages in second-rate magazines." He put George Meredith easily at the head of the later novelists. He found the *Earthly Paradise* " a singularly primitive, unaffected story, which gave me no headwork and very little heartache." But when somebody gave him *The Epic of Hades*, he merely supposed that the young men in England did not know what a good book was since they could " praise such stuff." He did not like Popery and said it " almost destroys poetry." From the generalization he proceeds to the particular statement that in our older literature there is no good papist poet, instances Habington in support of his argument, and overlooks Southwell and Crashaw. He sometimes touched an out-of-the-way poet, and recommends to a correspondent " a beautiful old poem, Tickell's *Elegy on Addison*." He thought that Campbell would outlive

---

gives a pleasant account of the informal classes in Hampstead, at which Cory gave instruction in the classics to Mary Coleridge and a few other women pupils.

Shelley. He seldom gave expression to less particular opinions about literature; we but rarely get notes such as—" If there is one kind of literature that I hate more than another, it is ingenious interpretation of the Bible; worse than Gladstone on Homer."

V.

His opinions on life in general are frequently full of point and admirably turned. " I wish people would everywhere take up the pretty etiquette of presenting a guest on his departure with a nosegay. It would be much more pleasing than the sandwiches which one gets nowadays," the humour of which is recalled by another remark that " the lieutenants were as dull as cricketers." His wish that " the British monarchy would similarly pass away with Victoria " is a little unexpected from so devoted a loyalist—one who had written in his Eton days when a small boy had mocked as he was talking to a class about the Queen's marriage: " Her Majesty is the only topic upon which I can tolerate no difference of opinion." His mind was of the curious Tory-Liberal blend that is common in the finest English character. He was all for the State and constitution, and yet he could write half humorously, but half seriously: " I have thought the nations would jar less and the cities would be liker to temples, if government were entrusted to young couples in their first year of wed-lock. The happiness of the months just before and

after marriage is perhaps an equivalent for wisdom."
Youth and death kept a constant fellowship in his
mind. He exulted in the one, and was brave in contemplation of the other: " The Universities are Highland reservoirs of spring waters gathered, the springs
of youth;" and then: " Was death invented that there
might be poetry? If so after all it is not so senseless
an arrangement." And he could turn with ease from
the clear thinking of " every character described by
literature becomes the germs of characters and fragments of characters " to the whimsical—

" Other Germans . . . when not speaking of England, gave me satisfaction; and I regret more than
ever that their language is indigestible. ' Herz ' and
' Schmerz ' rhyme (or rime) twelve times in their version
of *Africaine*, and when Vasco said, at the end of his
song, ' Unsterblichkeit ' with the South German slush-
ing of the guttural, it was truly nauseous."

VI.

Although he lived to be seventy, Cory's views and
intellectual position were hardly modified after he
turned fifty, and when he died he would probably
have stood by a little confession he wrote in a letter
of 1875:

" After so much tossing to and fro I cast anchor on
Tennyson as the representative of Virgil, on France as
the representative of Augustan Rome, on Darwin as
wiser than Mill, on the law and the science of my own
time, of my own nation, which gathers up and does

justice to all the products of German penetration, on the synthesis of English and French thought, on republics, once more glorified by Victor Hugo and Swinburne. This last is the only extravagance or vehemence, I think, that has any charm for me. . . ."

Indeed, some years before he was fifty he seems to have thought of himself as settled in age. "My Eton song is finished and copied out. . . . It is a failure, and I must be content with prose. Too old for verse; the little slender vein is worked out. But I have my readers like better men." But his mind never became vague, nor, except in so far as all political thinking is beset by the curse, was he ever given to easy generalization. The breadth of his learning and human sympathy was always sharpened by meticulousness as to detail, even to the point of noting among much more impressive matter that he had been lecturing " on *Is qui* with subjunctive." It is perhaps fanciful to suppose that this habit of mind was in some way connected with his defective eyesight, but the psychological cause and effect of these things is sometimes odd in this way. When he was forty-four he notes: "Coming back up the moor by sunset I saw, to my delight, a live bird perched on a wall, just in time with my glasses. . . . I hardly ever saw a free bird before—it was a great pleasure," and elsewhere he speaks of the movement of a cow's forelegs as being one of the most graceful things in nature. There is something almost of insensitiveness, wholly unexpected from him, and perhaps the more so because of his own affliction, in an Egyptian travel note, when he says: "Moreover, I wish there were not so many blinking, dull eyes. I don't mind a sprinkling of real blind folk, whose presence in the crowded lanes is a precious sign of the people's gentleness, but the amaurosis is mean and dismal." The only other occasion where there is an ineptness of the same character in his journals, though it is in a different context altogether, is when he speaks of the Downs of Needles Bay as being "quite as elastic and much loftier than those at Bude." These things are trivial, but they may be noted without offence in a character that was of singular purity and sureness. In nothing, perhaps, does Cory's essential goodness—to use a somewhat discredited word in its simple meaning—show itself more sweetly than in its love of music. This was a life-long passion with him, and when it was on him he was apt to rate everything else as of little account:

"Life without music is despicable, with it inexplicably strange. . . . Listening to pathetic songs I rebel against the death of those who sang them in the old times: the makers of those melodies are my unknown brethren; all others who speak in what we call words fail to let me know them thoroughly; music is the only communion of hearts, and it makes one's heart feel hopelessly empty."

In 1872, he writes in a letter:

". . . Mozart gives me the sense of perfect angelic freedom, like the best parts of our 1790–1860 poetry;

like the pretty movement in *Christabel*, in Tennyson's *Maud*, in Keats's *Hyperion*.

"What I should like to be told is that Gluck lived to hear Mozart's best things well performed, and rejoiced in being surpassed and *fulfilled*, and to wish Virgil could hear them."

In another place he notes that "my journals have many a bit of romance about tunes," and as a final example of his musical enthusiasm may be given his note on the violin, which is in particular to him, he says, "a symbol of infinity, not bounded by a keyboard, not divisible into the octaves—one can imagine it in another world, keeping its identity but endlessly extending its range and taking our ears along with it."

Perhaps in place of a peroration it will be more fitting to take leave of our poet, himself so little rhetorical, with a story told by him with many others, with his own charm of humorous appreciation. It is an anecdote of Queen Victoria, who had apparently been doubtful about the marriage of a certain Dean and was ultimately reconciled to it. She "joined the hands of the Dean and his lady and said to him: 'Never forsake her, don't forget her, don't leave her behind on the platform.'"

VII.

The following six hitherto unpublished letters, now in my possession, are given as an Appendix to this paper. They were written by Cory in January and February, 1891, less than six months before his death, to Mr. Julian Marshall, the connoisseur and collector. They have the interest of being concerned with Cory's own writings. I have attached a few explanatory notes in square brackets. Cory's idosyncrasy in punctuation is retained.

Letter I.

[The 1877 pamphlet, *Ionica II*, is now very scarce. When Cory gave it away " for a shilling a copy privately," as he puts it, he was in the habit of correcting two or three misprints. My own copy is so marked.

H. A. J. Munro, of Trinity College, Cambridge, was Kennedy Professor of Latin from 1869 to 1872.]

" 25, Cannon Place, N.W.
" *January* 19, 1891.

" Dear Sir,—I send the privately printed pamphlet of 1877 which was meant originally for two or three friends and was put forth with many absurd errors due to my own carelessness—of this thing there are a good many copies in a drawer here

" Of the original *Ionica* there are no bound copies. Rain of Haymarket and Bowes of Macmillan's shop Cambridge took some few years ago all the sheets which my brother discovered in his house of which I was the tenant.

" When Mr Bain told me in 1890 that he had sold his last copy and that there was a demand I with some misgivings took measures for publishing in order to save trouble or doubt to my executors.

" The agent employed has had the poor booklet badly printed, and I myself was careless in looking at the proofs

" My friends have pointed out to me ' tyrranous ' and croppres—(croppies) and I have observed (besides heart for art) ' doubt ' for ' doat ' on p 184 l 10

" I daresay there are other slips

" As you say you are curious about obscure books I venture to say that there is an obscure schoolbook Lucretilis published by Ingalton Drake of Eton College which was in writing declared by the late leader of English Latinists H. A. J. Munro to be the *only* good imitation of Horace The *Key* to this schoolbook gives my Latin and I, who am no judge, like that Latin well enough to read it. I tried to imitate Horace in a scrap about Britomart and I have printed in magazines seven or eight sets of *Rhymes after Horace*

" I am yours faithfully
" WM. CORY "

LETTER II.

[The Rhymes after Horace to which Cory refers in these letters do not seem to have been recovered from the magazines. Reference to tne files of Murray's and Macmillan's of that time show that his contributions were as follows: Murray's: October, 1889, *Licymnia* (Hor. *Od.* ii. 12); December, 1889, *Achilles* (Hor. *Epod.* xiii.). Macmillan's: August, 1888, *Rhymes after Horace*, *Neæra* (Hor. *Epod.* xv.), *Asterie* (Hor. *Od.* iii. 7); September, 1889, *Rhymes after Horace*, *Phyllis I.* (Hor. *Od.* ii. 4), *II.* (Hor. *Od.* iv. 11). These were variously attributed to *Ofella, Ofellus*, and *To the Author of Ionica*.

Cory was always emphatic from the first that his poem should not have won the Chancellor's medal in competition with Maine's.]

"January 20, 1891.

" Dear Sir—Mr Ingalton Drake Publisher Eton College Windsor probably has copies of the Key to Lucretilis at 2/ a piece and will sell one to anyone but an Eton schoolboy—he would recognise my name — You would hardly care for the English translations which was/is used by boys learning how to make ' Lyrics.' I think this costs 2/ I should never have attached any value to the booklet but for Munro's surprising letter — he gave me as a reward a copy of his Horace which I always use in Lessons (gratis lessons) with ladies

" The Magazines to which I sent my rhymes after Horace were Murray's and Macmillan's in 1888 or 1889 — I kept for myself only manuscript copies some of which are in a book first employed in the keeping of Calverley's Soracte Bandusia Leuconoe etc

" The things I sent to the Magazine were Asterie Neæra* Phyllis (ne sit ancillae) Phyllis Est mihi nonum Licymnia. I did not send a ' Donec Gratus Eram ' which I did long ago at the request of a Newnham lady nor Barine (C J Foxs favourite Ode) which being now printed is by a well read Cambridge man taken to be a tribute to a *Russian* lady of fast habits

" Amongst the things kept back I have a 40 line thing in blank verse which I made for a literary lady — her father showed it to Lord Tennyson — it is a translation of a bit of Euripides Supplices giving five characters of slain warriors. I sent through a Cambridge friend to a Cambridge Magazine about 18 months ago a bit of Aeneid the March of Camilla in blank verse done like other things in usum virginum

" Dr Whewell was very courteous to me in 1843

* *Epodes.*

when he gave the imprimatur to my Plato which got
the medal that was really due to a beautiful precious
poem of Maine's I often show Maine's, my own never.
" I am yours gratefully
" WM CORY "

" I treat ' Ionica II ' as waste paper. I cant imagine
it told by itself."

LETTER III.

[Cecil Spring-Rice was Sir Cecil Arthur Spring-Rice,
who died in 1918, and was latterly British Ambassador
at Washington. The voyage referred to was during
Cory's Egyptian travels with the Countess of Win-
chelsea and her sons. The ship was the *Ceylon*, and
Cory in his Journal gives a graphic account of a storm
in the Bay of Biscay, when the behaviour of the Captain
(Evans) provoked his unbounded admiration. A
Captain Rice is also spoken of.]

" 25, CANNON PLACE, N.W.
" February 7, 1891.

" MY DEAR SIR,—I have found Macmillan's Magazine September 1889—its cover states that it contains
Rhymes after Horace by Ofellus, but I have long ago
torn out the pages thus indicated and given them to
someone — I believe they were Asterie and Neæra
i.e.   Quid fles Asterie and Nox erat et coelo
" I retain them in my own writing in an old
copybook, and if you like I can lend you the copybook
The then editor of Macmillan's Magazine Mowbray
Morris was formerly in my class at Eton   *not my pupil*
he preserved his anonymity with a stately recognition
of my identity and I rank him in my curiosities of
literature The Editor of Murray, now a publisher,

was my pupil for a short time. Neither of these potentates expressed a wish for continuance of my tribute

" I should never have attempted rhyming after Horace had I not been asked by my pupil Eva Hugessen to try ' Donec Gratus ' which she had tried

" I imagine you are akin to another pupil of mine Cecil Spring Rice whom I knew as a little boy and have heard of since he grew up — In January 1873 I was on board ship with a kinsman of his, a Marshall who had been at Eton with me though junior to me —with him I had pleasant chats in the Mediterranean

" I venture to offer you, as you deign to take interest in my things, the loan of my copy of Lucretilis as it has short notes as to the origin of some of the things — I am more egotistical about that humble schoolbook than about anything else — at least I have a sneaking wish that it may escape the fate of my other things and last a little longer.

" As to Plato I am a mere dabbler but I have helped several women in Phaedo, Apologia, Phaedrus, Georgias, Symposium, Theætetus

" I remain yours very truly
" WM CORY "

LETTER IV.

[The autograph *Pour Rire* is as follows. It is written by Cory, as was his custom, without punctuation, the spaces being left to denote pauses, and it is so printed here.

Pour Rire.

" Mat Prior   diplomat and wit
In Paris   in the Opera pit
next to a Marquis chanced to sit

Well sang the tenor   and the lord
hummed   as he fancied   in accord
and by the humming Mat was bored.
Between two acts the ape would chat
So turning   and accosting Mat
he said   ' a splendid tenor that '
Mat would not give the man his due.
' damn him.'   ' Why damn him ?'   ' O Moseu
' he sings so loud I can't hear you.'

With this is a Limerick which is hardly worth printing.]

" February 9, 1891.

" My Dear Sir—I send by post a little copybook started first for Calverley — it contains rough copies of the 2 Phyllis that went to McMillan, and other scraps

" I add an autograph pour rire   There are—naturally—sundries in my copybooks and flyleaves—some things have perished   My heir will probably not care for what I wish to save, sundry bits of Greek turned from English

" I am proud of having been, long ago so lucky as to do a bit of Latin which went into a schoolbook that I have never even seen, called folia silvulae or silvulae-foliorum or both—' reviewed ' in a paper—my scrap was I believe quoted—so it was seen by Tennyson, and in his autograph I saw that he called my version of his ' Hesper ' exquisite.   So I valued that scrap at least (principibus placuisse)

" I am
" Yours very truly
" Wm Cory

" 25 Cannon Place, N.W."

LETTER V.

[*Gemini and Virgo*, one of Calverley's most celebrated pieces, appeared in *Verses and Translations*, first published in 1862. William George Clarke, joint editor of the Cambridge Shakespeare, was Public Orator at Cambridge from 1857 to 1870, and endowed the Clarke Lectureship in English Literature at Trinity.]

" *February* 16 (1891).

" MY DEAR SIR—The parcel containing my two relics and the four valuable volumes that you give me arrived just now and caught me at home.

" I have been away and shall be again

" I have in former years bought to give away some Calverley, and borrowed other Calverley, and I have known enough of him to enable me to think of him and sometimes talk of him. I shall be glad to go all through the four volumes and I hope I may live to read Theocritus once more—with ladies—under his guidance.

" My wife tells me that I very seldom smile but I know that I laugh often, and laugh heartily *when alone*. This is a guarantee against madness.

" Gemini and Virgo amused many a boy in my little room a quarter of a century ago.

" The last Calverleys that I copied were in a recent Cambridge collection of merry rhymes of which I forget the title, and I thought of the author when I was in Cambridge last July. The wit of *my* Cambridge in the early forties was W. G. Clarke, he got the prize in our ' Epigram Club ' with a poem infinitely too long to be called an epigram. About a Proctor chased by his own bulldogs.

" Rendering hearty thanks for your gift I remain dear Sir

" Yours sincerely
" WM CORY "

LETTER VI.

[Calverley's *Fly Leaves* was first published in 1872. *The Back-Slider and Other Poems*, by Antaeus, was published in 1890, and is by a poet who is less known than he should be—W. J. Ibbett. Frankland Lushington was probably Franklin Lushington, Accountant-General of Madras, who published some martial verses, *Points of War*, in 1855. The note from Richard Burton, enclosed by Cory, is as follows:

" REID'S, *Jan.* 4.

" DEAR SIR,—With great pleasure on Saturday—if possible. Please remind Madame of the Carne [?] e altro. Many thanks for the loan of the book. I have only dipped into it. Before Franschio's day electricity was used at the Castle of [?] near Trieste and V. Hugo mentions this in the ' Travailleurs de la Mer.'

" I am dear Sir
" Very truly yours
" WILLIAM CORY, ESQ."   " R. F. BURTON.

In 1881 Cory had written from Madeira to Lord Esher: " Madame (his wife) is quite a Calypso to the R.N. captains, and her last conquest is that real Ulysses, Captain Burton, the Mahommedan, would-be Mormon, etc."]

"DEAR SIR,—Yes. I duly received the two things returned by you. I have been feasting on Flyleaves with more wonder than ever. I perceive that I once had the honour of being in a volume with Calverley. He was asked, it seems by Mont. Butler to translate into verse (Latin) as I into Greek verse Lord Carlisle's lines about Lady St. German's tree—the tiny thing is called ' Flebilis Arbor ' I think I never read such good biographical writing as Seeley's reminiscences of Calverley

"Some anonymous poet has sent to anonymous me through Geo. Allen, a libellus of 20 pages called ' Backslider ' by Antaeus, printed (100 copies) for the author sold by Elkin Mathews Vigo Street W They are more interesting to me than the lately lent volumes of Robert Bridges and Mrs Woods, but far less than Sir Alfred Lyall's.

" ' To a dead Mistress ' seems to me original and clever, and it might have been printed in a magazine

"A friend of mine seems to have resumed an old project that he and I made long ago, to print a set of poems of all sorts of writers for barrack libraries under the title Sabretasch and I have just tried to remember the things about soldiership that I have read Amongst these are two written by my Cambridge friend Frankland Lushington who was in [word illegible] and perhaps still is—to my disgust his ' Cabul ' did not get the Chancellor's medal

"I am dear Sir

"Yours sincerely

"WM. CORY.

"Would you like to have a note written by Sir Richard Burton, he was worth seeing . . . ten years ago "

NOTE.

The preceding paper brought me a courteous letter from Captain Drummond of Winchester. This gentleman is the A. H. Drummond of the *Letters and Journals* of 1897, where are to be found a few of his letters from Cory, of which he subsequently placed in my hands the entire series, amounting to a considerable volume; giving me leave to copy them and, so far as he is concerned, to publish such extracts from them as I may wish. This, perhaps, I may do at some other time. He also wrote, " I send you a copy of a poem which he [Cory] gave me to read in 1873 when staying with him at Halsdon." This poem has not hitherto been published, and I am indebted to Captain Drummond for the opportunity of printing it here. There is more heavy going in it than was common in Cory's verse, but there is also enough of his fastidious phrasing to make it welcome to the select body of Cory's admirers.

MIDNIGHT.

How long, ye patient stars, how long
Will ye keep leaning down to gaze
On this poor toy of changeful days ?
 Listening, listening still
 All our sounds of ill;
 The groans of writhing doubt,
 Hope's dirge, and passion's rout;
Listening the weary wail of our old prison song.

 Think ye not scorn to throw a beam
 Into our sobbing ocean stream,

Upon the shivering waves to risk
The one-ness of each burning disk,
To let the vapour rise between
Your glances and our nether scene;
And when the wind that lifts the cloud
Through the chill enfolding night,
Strips the dead worldlet of its shroud,
Opened piecemeal into sight;
Then to look down with that calm, ghostly sheen;
Then once again to send so far
The ray we slight, the smile we mar,
Then to make peace more deep and silence more serene.

In holy vigils, far apart, repose
More orbal substances of yellow fire;
And they are waiting till our planet goes
All sin and pain to its own funeral pyre:
And we beneath those myriad eyes,
Forgetting that they mutely chide
The stirrings of our lust and pride,
Build on the thought that we are wise;
And, by the jargon of our boast,
Blush not to tell that awful host,
How false we are to their realities !

Our thoughts are all at war, our plans
Stretch out, as if the whole were man's,
As if we only claimed to be
Lords of that distant galaxy:
And still, while over-daring hope
Shoots up beneath the heavenly cope,
We vaunt, and fight, and play a game
Of idle toils for idle fame;
And they the silent worlds look down,
    Oh not in scorn,
Too wise to smile, too fair to frown
    Most like to them that mourn.

At the end of the MS. is Cory's note as follows:

" These lines were written at Cambridge about the year 1843; and, after the lapse of twenty years, found in a drawer, and copied out without altering. *Jan : * 17, 1864."

PATRICK BRANWELL BRONTË
AND HIS "HORACE"

PATRICK BRANWELL BRONTË
AND HIS "HORACE"

I

PATRICK BRANWELL BRONTË died in 1848, at the age of thirty-one. Little celebrated for any achievement of his own, he is a not unfamiliar figure to students of the ever-increasing volume of Brontë literature. Through the life-story of his more famous sisters, already sufficiently tragic in itself, his failure of character sounds, perhaps, the most unhappy note of all. The scourge of disease that destroyed the family, and the incessant problem of ways and means, could be faced with a greater fortitude than the constant betrayal of the hopes that were centred in a brother at once highly gifted, beloved, and incurably weak in fibre. Most of the biographers and critics have been agreed upon the matter, and the evidence is plain enough. Branwell made a mess of his life, and he was a cause of great suffering to three brave and devoted women. When drink and opium made an end —or hastened it, since by the latter he died of consumption like the others—natural affection can but have been conscious of a deep anxiety gone. But, while bad remains bad, there are aspects of the badness in this case that have, perhaps, been overlooked by Branwell's detractors.

Formal acknowledgment has generally been made of

his gifts; they have even been allowed to have been brilliant. Mrs. Gaskell tells us how among the children, all pretty much of an age, busily writing their poems and romances, it was the brother who by common consent was to bring fame to the family; she adds, on her own account: "He was very clever, no doubt; perhaps to begin with, the greatest genius in this rare family." We are told that his wit and talent were sought for the entertainment of strangers by the land-lord of the " Black Bull " at Haworth, in return for a share in the bottle. Other writers, speaking in censure, have nevertheless allowed that the disaster of Branwell's life was the more miserable because of the promise betrayed. What this promise actually was we are not so clearly told. Mrs. Gaskell quotes only one fragment of his juvenile verse. It is not notable, but the poor opinion that the biographer expresses of it would be more convincing if she had not already given an equally indifferent specimen of Charlotte's writing as showing " remarkable poetical talent." When the sisters published their book of poems in 1846, Branwell's work was not included, though it almost certainly must have been known to them, and was, in flashes, better than anything that the book contained with the exception of Emily's best poems.* Francis A. Leyland, in *The Brontë Family*† gave several

* The reason may well have been that the sisters, in their desire for pseudonymity, could not trust Branwell with the secret.

† *The Brontë Family, with special Reference to Patrick Branwell Brontë*, by Francis A. Leyland. Two volumes. Hurst and Blackett,

examples of his work, which did not reappear in book
form until Mr. A. C. Benson included a very clumsily
edited selection in his *Brontë Poems* of 1915. Mr.
Benson's Introduction pays a qualified tribute to
Branwell's "instinct for poetry," and a yet more
qualified one to his expression. This was, perhaps,
all that could be asked; it was, in any case, nearer
justice than the merely uncritical petulance of Mary
F. Robinson and some other writers. The poems
recovered, carelessly enough, by Mr. Benson, had no
more than traces of genius. But they had that.
Noah's Warning over Methuselah's Grave and some
twenty lines scattered among the other poems, were
not enough to call up more than the ghost of a reputation for Branwell. But they are very good in themselves, and they have this interest: they are tokens of
the something in him that gave rise to the tradition
of his rare gifts that survives from the family records.

The cherished hope for Branwell, however, was not
as a poet but as a painter. When he was eighteen
he was to be sent to the Royal Academy School, but the
scheme came to nothing. Yet here, again, we hear of

1886.—Leyland's book is the most important plea that has been made
for Branwell. Mr. Shorter, than whom the sisters have had no more
devoted and generous student, but who shares the common inability
to see any good in Branwell, dismisses the book as merely dull. I
don't find it that. It is loosely put together, and it must be allowed
that Leyland was no oracle upon literature. But I find it a very
readable and informing book. It is also an extremely inconvenient
one for the prosecution.

great promise, but when an occasional reference to
performance is made, it is disparaging. And again, the
evidence, slight though it is, is against disparagement.
I have in my possession one of the touching little
Haworth manuscripts, a play called *Caractacus*, written
by Branwell in 1830, when he was thirteen. It has
the charming colophon: " Begun June 26, Ended June
28. A.D. 1830. Therefore I have Finished It in 2 days
Sunday wich happened between being left out P. B.
Brontë." The play has unusual constructive power
for a child, otherwise it is what we should look for in
expression. But it is embellished with two or three
marginal sketches that show a decided talent for
drawing, and, moreover, the pages themselves are
set out with a quite attractive sense of design. But
of much greater importance is the portrait that
Branwell painted of his three sisters, when he was
older but still well under twenty. Mr. Benson uses it
as a frontispiece to his edition, as an interesting record,
but in speaking only of its roughness and " unskilled
handling " he follows Mrs. Gaskell, who thinks that the
likenesses are admirable, but that it was " not much
better than sign-painting (there are signs and signs)
as to manipulation," and again refers to the " good
likenesses, however badly executed." Loving Charlotte as she did, it is not surprising that Mrs.
Gaskell did not like what she knew of Branwell—she
never met him—but her affections at least did not
sharpen what was, perhaps, no great natural acumen
as an art critic. The painting is in the National

Portrait Gallery, and a moment's inspection of it shows it to be, as the production of an almost untutored boy,* remarkable in more than promise. It has charming qualities of colour, design and characterization, immature but unmistakable. When, however, we pass from this to Branwell's later portrait of Emily, painted some ten years afterwards, immaturity has gone, and we are in the presence of startling achievement. Mr. Milner, the Director of the National Portrait Gallery, tells me that he and his predecessor, Sir Charles Holmes, have always looked upon the picture, since it was bought in 1914, as one of the most beautiful things in the collection. It has the simple tenderness of a Primitive in tone and colour, and it is admirably designed and drawn. As a revelation of Emily's character, moreover, it is astonishing. The stormy power of *Wuthering Heights* blends with the premonitions of approaching death. The portrait gives Branwell a modest place among the little masters. And yet even in this connection his assailants have refused to admit plain evidence. They merely betray an ignorance of what painting is, but it is amusing to speculate as to what they would have said if this could have been shown to be Charlotte's work instead of Branwell's.†

* About this time Charlotte and Branwell were receiving lessons from William Robinson, an artist, of Leeds.

† An interesting point arises on looking at these portraits, as Mr. Milner suggests. Following Mrs. Gaskell's description of the group, it has been accepted always that Charlotte is on the right of the picture

This, then, is the figure hitherto presented of the
" contemptible caitiff " pilloried by Swinburne, whose
moral indignations were sometimes the least impressive
things about a great poet and a great gentleman. We
find a sensitive and affectionate child, growing with
charm into boyhood, talented by report rather than
by admitted evidence, drifting into a dissolute young
manhood, a drunkard, a sponge, " culpably negligent "
in his employment, acquiring " all the cunning of the
opium eater," and wasting himself into a miserable
and early death. That is the story as we have it,
and, so far as it goes, it is clear. On the whole,
Charlotte's letters must be allowed to outweigh even
Leyland's testimony. But is there, perhaps, another
side of the story that has not been very carefully
considered ? We have been told, and rightly, that
Branwell was a disaster to his family. He cannot be
absolved from that lamentable indecision of soul that
makes love a bitterness. But even the worst case is
never quite so simple as it seems. Is there not something to be said for considering also the disaster that
he was to himself, and how it came about ?

Of Branwell's misused talent more is to be said
later. For the moment I wish to think a little

---

as we look at it, Emily in the centre, and Anne on the left. But on
comparing it with the later single portrait of Emily, the authenticity
of which was vouched for by Mr. Nicholls, Charlotte's husband, there
seems to be little doubt that Emily is the figure on the left, with
Anne in the centre. Mrs. Gaskell had never seen either Emily or
Anne.

more closely of the failure of character, but in order
to do this I must take it for granted in advance that
he had a real strain of the poet in him, that the family
tradition was well founded, as I hope to show clearly
it was.   We remember, then, that he was the one boy
in a bleak north country vicarage, with no mother,
and a father who seems to have been fond but uncertain
of temper and not very effective;* the brother of

* The Rev. Patrick Brontë, too, made verses, sometimes wonder-
fully:
> O ! when shall we see our dear Jesus,
> His presence from poverty frees us. . . .

His *Cottage Poems* (1811) breathe an atmosphere of devastating pious-
ness, but there lingers in them something of the eighteenth-century
deportment, and in one or two, for example the *Winter Night Meditations* (published by Longman, separately and anonymously in 1810
as *Winter Evening Thoughts*), there is a real touch of Crabbe's power.

> The prostitute with faithless smiles,
> Remorseless plays her tricks and wiles.
> Her gesture bold, and ogling eye,
> Obtrusive speech, and pert reply,
> And brazen front, and stubborn tone,
> Shew all her native virtue's flown.
>   *   *   *   *   *
> And, now, she practises the art,
> Which snared her unsuspecting heart;
>   *   *   *   *   *
> Averse to good, and prone to ill,
> And dexterous in seducing skill;
> To look, as if her eyes would melt;
> T' affect a love, she never felt. . . .

The preface, however, must be a unique monument of self-satisfaction,
and Mr. Brontë was doubtless rather a discouraging person to live with.

three sisters whose rare moral sureness of touch was
uncertain just in the one matter of looking upon any
incipient weakness in him as a sign of budding manli-
ness. It is no excuse for him to say that he was spoilt
as a child, but it is to begin to understand something
about him. Charlotte and Anne were not poets,
Emily and Branwell were. These two had the wildness, the sense of loneliness, the ache for some indefin-
able thing called freedom, that mark the poet from
infancy. The Haworth parsonage was bad lodging
for such spirits. Emily found her escape from it on
the moors, Branwell his in the " Black Bull." His was
a bad choice as it happened. He had not the resistance that thrives in taverns, and he was at once on
easy terms with temptation. But it is not difficult
to see why he was so early ripe for temptation when
it came his way.

He spent hours over a map of London until he knew
every street and byway in the city, and was able to tell
a stranger at the inn of short cuts from Charing Cross,
say, to Holborn. " My aim, sir," he wrote, when he
was nineteen, to Wordsworth, " is to push out into the
open world." He had been assured by all the opinion
he knew, at home and in the village, that he was to
make a great name. Nobody seems to have gone
beyond this to stiffen resolution in himself to make it,
and consumption was at work upon his vitality. He
loved literature, and he was no poor scholar, as will be
shown. It was this boy, sensitive, ambitious, flattered,
diseased in a household of disease, who suddenly had

placed before him the romantic adventure of going to London to study art. Mrs. Gaskell, wantonly as it seems to me, suggests that part of the attraction was that " he would have a license of action only to be found in crowded cities." Here, at least, he might have had the benefit of the doubt. A temperament like Branwell's in youth is, on the whole, more likely to save itself in the release and preoccupations of London than in the restrictions of Haworth. London was the El Dorado of his imagination, not necessarily a vicious one, and he cared very much about a career in one or another of the arts. The enchanting project fell through. He did not go to the Royal Academy, and, save for a short and hopeless effort to make a living in Bradford in competition with the established artists, he did not become a painter by profession. He became, instead, in turn an usher, a private tutor, and a clerk on the Leeds and Manchester Railway.

It might have been expected to pacify Branwell's critics to reflect, from all the available evidence, that if for the short ten years of his manhood he was a great trial to his sisters, he was desperately unhappy himself. It was his own fault, no doubt, but the adage serves. His ambitions were defeated; his hunger for intellectual society was satisfied only by a stray acquaintance on his few visits to Manchester or Liverpool; he chafed in his routine employments as sorely as has many a young man of more effective spirit and determination. He was often at home without the society of his sisters, who were now spending much of their time away as school-

teachers, and even when he had not to be alone in
what must have been a cheerless home, we may be
allowed to wonder whether the companionship of
Charlotte, at least, for all her affection, was a very
happy one for him. She bore much, and heroically,
but there is a grim little story in Leyland of an occasion
when Branwell, by a small errand of mercy, made an
attempted return to grace. He had done his best,
but had failed in his mission, and was miserable about
it. He told Charlotte. " She looked at me with a
look I shall never forget. . . . It was not like her at
all. . . . It was a dubious look. It ran over me,
questioning, and examining, as if I had been a wild
beast. . . . It said, ' I wonder if that's true ?' But,
as she left the room, she seemed to accuse herself of
having wronged me, (and) smiled kindly upon me. . . .
When she was gone I came over here to the ' Black
Bull,' and made a note of it in sheer disgust and
desperation. Why could they not give me some
credit when I was trying to be good ?" It is not a
pleasing picture that Branwell gives of himself, but
there is a touch of tragic colour in the story that does
not come wholly from his own frailties.

He further became involved in a wretched love
affair, that had neither health nor hope in it, and so the
unhappy tale went on, to-day perhaps with a sheriff's
officer at the door on a visit to B. inviting him either
to pay his debts or to take a trip to York, to-morrow
finding consolation in reading of the latest pugilistic
heroes in *Bell's Life* at the " Black Bull." And all the

time the aspirations of the young poet were smoulder-
ing, the care for things of good report persisting.
"He possessed then a familiar and extensive acquaintance with the Greek and Latin authors. He knew
well the history and condition of Europe, and of this
country, in past and present times," says Leyland.
It was not common stuff that was drifting to ruin.
And he knew with a sad bitterness what was happening.
"My heartfelt thanks to you," he writes at the conclusion of one of his letters, "for your consideration
for one who has none for himself." At the end,
according to the account given by Mrs. Gaskell, which,
although it is disputed by Leyland, I hope is true,
a moment of his beloved Emily's stubborn courage came
to him out of some recess of his nature. "I have
heard, from one who attended Branwell in his last illness, that he resolved on standing up to die. He had
repeatedly said that as long as there was life there was
strength of will to do what it chose; and when the last
agony began, he insisted on assuming the position just
mentioned." Branwell was a tragedy to his sisters,
but in his heart there may have been an even deeper
tragedy than theirs.

II.

The extant poems of Branwell Brontë, with three
exceptions,* are to be found in Leyland, and in various
manuscripts. Of the last the most considerable is

* Printed in Mrs. Oliphant's *William Blackwood and his Sons*,
(1897).

that printed for the first time in 1924. It consists of a complete translation, written out entirely in Branwell's own hand, of the first book of Horace's Odes, omitting the last, of which he says: "This Ode I have no heart to attempt, after having heard Mr. H. Coleridge's translation, on May Day, at Ambleside."* The manuscript is signed at the end, "P. B. Brontë," and dated "Haworth, Nr. Bradford, Yorks, June 27, 1840." On New Year's Day of that year, he had gone to Broughton-in-Furness, on the edge of the Lake District, as tutor in the family of a Mr. Postlethwaite, and he returned to Haworth in June, so that most of the translations were presumably made while he held that appointment. He was twenty-three years of age at the time. Just as the portrait of Emily is the most convincing proof of his gifts as a painter, so these translations seem to me to be his best achievement, so far as we can judge, as a poet. They are unequal,

---

* Hartley Coleridge's translation of Book I., Ode xxxviii., is as follows:

> Nay, nay, my boy—'tis not for me,
> This studious pomp of eastern luxury:
> Give me no various garlands—fine
>   With linden twine,
> Nor seek, where latest lingering blows
>   The solitary rose.
> Earnest I beg—add not, with toilsome pain,
> One far-sought blossom to the myrtle plain,
> For sure, the fragrant myrtle bough
>   Looks seemliest on thy brow;
> Nor me mis-seems, while, underneath the vine,
> Close interweaved, I quaff the rosy wine.

and they have many of the bad tricks of writing that
come out of some deeply rooted defect of character.
But they also have a great many passages of clear lyrical
beauty, and they have something of the style that
comes from a spiritual understanding, as apart from
merely formal knowledge, of great models.

Horace has been a favourite mark for English trans-
lators, including many of our more considerable poets.
Jonson, Cowley, Milton, Dryden, Pope, Prior, Con-
greve, Calverley—these and others have done occasionally what less famous writers have done systematically,
and it cannot be said that on the whole they have
done it any better. Cowley may bring off a line like

> And trusts the faithless April of thy May,

or Dryden—

> The half unwilling willing kiss,

but they are no surer of making a good poem in translation than the Creeches and the Sewells. And that
is the only test. If you know Latin, you don't want
an English translation of Horace unless into the bargain
you get a good English poem; if you don't know Latin
(as I don't), still you want the translation only on the
same terms. Horace has been responsible for some
good English poems, and a great many dull ones.
Even Ben Jonson, in his translation *The Art of
Poetry* (1640), in spite of a few splendid phrases, such
as "The deeds of Kings, great Captains, and sad
wars," strangely demonstrates for the most part what
poetry is not, and, as a later translator, Henry Ames,

protests in 1727, "has trod so close upon the Heels of
Horace, that he has not only crampt, but made him
halt in (almost) every line." The Earl of Roscommon's
translation (1680) in blank verse gives the sense but
little else. And so also it is generally with the Odes.
Among the more or less complete translations are
those of Sir Thomas Hawkins (1625, with later enlarged
editions), Thomas Creech (1684), and miscellanies
such as Alexander Brome's (1666), and Jacob Tomson's
(1715), containing translations by various hands. In
later days we have W. Sewell (1850), John Conington
(1863-1869), and Sir Theodore Martin (1860).
Scattered about these volumes are several beautiful
versions of different poems, reasonably faithful to the
original,* and many more striking passages or stanzas.
Now we get Hawkins with

> no lot shall gaine
> Thee a King's Title in a Taverne-raigne;

and then Richard Fanshawe with

> What Stripling now thee discomposes
> In Woodbine Rooms, on Beds of Roses,

and again Creech, mildly, with

> But now I do repent the wrong
> And now compose a softer Song
>   To make Thee just amends.
> Recant the errors of my Youth
> And swear those scandals were not Truth;
>   So You and I be friends.

---

* There were the fashionable " Imitations " of the seventeenth and
eighteenth centuries, such as Prior's *Ode to Colonel George Villiers*,
which were freely topical adaptations.

Conington is, perhaps, the most consistently attractive
of them all, and he does make many of the Odes into
charming English verse. He often·strikes the note
as surely as in

> O lovelier than the lovely dame
>   That bore you, sentence as you please
> Those scurril verses, be it flame
>   Your vengeance craves, or Hadrian seas;

and no less an authority than Mr. A. E. Housman
tells me that he considers Conington's to be the
best English translations that he knows of Horace,
and as among the best verse translations in the
language.

Branwell Brontë's translations of the *First Book of
Odes* need, at their best, fear comparison with none.
They are not so uniformly good as Conington's, and
there are the ugly blemishes here and there of which
I have spoken. "Than thee" (XXIV.) is a lapse of
a less unpleasant kind than "gushing gore" (II.),
"swells my liver" and "boisterous bite" (XIII.).
Also, I think he occasionally mistranslates, as in XIX.
and XX., in the one of which he seems to be confused
as to the women and in the other as to the wines.
Sometimes, too, he chooses a bad measure, as in XII.
and XXXII., sometimes he is unexpectedly halting,
as in XXXI., and again flat or dull or heavy as in
XXVI., XXIX., XXXV., and XXXVII. Then there
are other cases where he just manages good average verse,
making it more interesting on the whole than most

of his competitors; XXVIII. is an instance. There remain more than half the Odes, of which it may be said that they are excellent in themselves, and as good as any English versions that I know, including Conington's. In a few instances I should say that they are decidedly the best of all. It is not only in frequent passages that Branwell sings with the right lyric ease, as in

> Yet—shuddering too at poverty
> Again he seeks that very sea—

and

> If but Euterpe yield to me
> Her thrilling pipe of melody,
> If Polyhymnia but inspire
> My spirit with her Lesbian lyre.
> Oh! Give thy friend a poet's name
> And heaven shall hardly bound his fame;

and

> O! brightest of his phalanx bright!
> With shining shoulders veiled from sight,
> Descend, Apollo Thou!

and many others (*e.g.*, the opening lines of the last stanza of IV.), but in some whole poems, as in the lovely rendering of XXI., there is hardly a flaw from beginning to end. At his best he has melody and phrase, and he builds his stanzas well. Further, he was happier in verse with Horace's subject-matter than he generally was with the experience of his own confused and frustrated life. I do not wish to advance any extravagant claim for this little book, but I think it adds appreciably to the evidence that Branwell Brontë was the second poet in his family, and a very good second at that, and that it leaves no justification for anyone again to say that he " composed nothing which gives him the slightest claim to the most inconsiderable niche in the temple of literature."

COLERIDGE, MILTON, AND WARTON

COLERIDGE, MILTON, AND WARTON

COLERIDGE spent the last eighteen years of his life, from 1816 to 1834, at the house of James Gillman, a surgeon of Highgate. The circumstances of his entering Gillman's household were remarkable. De Quincey, in one of his letters, asserted that Coleridge never gave up taking opium, and that he indulged the habit as a merely sensuous pleasure, being a man of sound health and constitution. The post-mortem examination held on Coleridge, at Gillman's instigation, revealed the fact that the poet must have for most of his life borne acute and more or less continuous suffering, and effectually disposed of the latter part of De Quincey's statement. Gillman himself asserted that the former part was equally unfounded, and his word is a convincing one.

In April, 1816, James Gillman, then living at Moreton House, Highgate, received an unusual request from a fellow medical practitioner. Dr. Joseph Adams of Hatton Garden, with whom Gillman had not more than the most casual acquaintance, wrote to the Highgate surgeon, on the ninth of that month, the following letter:

"Hatton Garden,
"9th *April*, 1816.

"Dear Sir,*

"A very learned, but in one respect an unfortunate gentleman, has applied to me on a singular occasion. He has for several years been in the habit of taking large quantities of opium. For some time past, he has been in vain endeavouring to break himself off it. It is apprehended his friends are not firm enough, from a dread, lest he should suffer by suddenly leaving it off, though he is conscious of the contrary; and has proposed to me to submit himself to any regimen, however severe. With this view, he wishes to fix himself in the house of some medical gentleman, who will have courage to refuse him any laudanum, and under whose assistance, should he be the worse for it, he may be relieved. As he is desirous of retirement, and a garden, I could think of no one so readily as yourself. Be so good as to inform me whether such a proposal is absolutely inconsistent with your family arrangements. I should not have proposed it, but on account of the great importance of the character, as a literary man. His communicative temper will make his society very interesting, as well as useful. Have the goodness to favour me with an immediate answer; and believe me, dear sir, your faithful humble servant,

"Joseph Adams."

Gillman informs us that he had seen Adams but twice, but that his interest was taken by the letter, and he determined to see the patient. On the evening of April 12, Coleridge accordingly presented himself at Highgate. He and Gillman took to each other at once.

* See Gillman's *Life of Samuel Taylor Coleridge*, 1838, p. 270.

Coleridge told Gillman about himself and confided in him his anxiety as to what would be the effect of discontinuing the habit. " He first informed me," says Gillman, " of the painful opinion which he had received concerning his case, especially from one medical man of celebrity. The tale was sad, and the opinion given unprofessional and cruel, sufficient to have deterred most men so afflicted from making the attempt Coleridge was contemplating, and in which his whole soul was so deeply and so earnestly engaged." Coleridge went away, and the next day wrote:

"42, NORFOLK STREET, STRAND,
"*Saturday Noon, April* 13, 1816.

" MY DEAR SIR,*
        " The first half hour I was with you convinced me that I should owe my reception into your family exclusively to motives not less flattering to me than honourable to yourself. I trust we shall ever in matters of intellect be reciprocally serviceable to each other. Men of sense generally come to the same conclusions; but they are likely to contribute to each other's enlargement of view, in proportion to the distance or even opposition of the points from which they set out. Travel and the strange variety of situations and employments on which chance has thrown me, in the course of my life, might have made me a mere man of *observation*, if pain and sorrow and self-miscomplacence had not forced my mind in on itself, and so formed habits of *meditation*. It is now as much my nature to evolve the fact from the law, as that of a practical man to deduce the law from the fact.

* See Gillman, p. 273.

" With respect to pecuniary remuneration, allow
me to say, I must not at least be suffered to make any
addition to your family expenses—though I cannot
offer anything that would be in any way adequate
to my sense of the service; for that indeed there could
not be a compensation, as it must be returned in kind,
by esteem and grateful affection.

" And now of myself. My ever-wakeful reason, and
the keenness of my moral feelings, will secure you from
all unpleasant circumstances connected with me save
only one, viz. the evasion of a specific madness. You
will never *hear* anything but truth from me: prior
habits render it out of my power to tell an untruth,
but unless carefully observed, I dare not promise that I
should not, with regard to this detested poison, be
capable of acting one. No sixty hours have yet passed
without my having taken laudanum, though for the
last week comparatively trifling doses. I have full
belief that your anxiety need not be extended beyond
the first week, I shall not, I must not be permitted to
leave your house, unless with you. Delicately or
indelicately, this must be done, and both the servants
and the assistant must receive absolute commands
from you. The stimulus of conversation suspends
the terror that haunts my mind; but when I am alone,
the horrors I have suffered from laudanum, the degra-
dation, the blighted utility, almost overwhelm me. If
(as I feel for the *first time* a soothing confidence it will
prove), I should leave you restored to my normal and
bodily health, it is not myself only that will love and
honour you; every friend I have (and thank God ! in
spite of this wretched vice I have many and warm
ones, who were friends of my youth, and have never
deserted me) will thank you with reverence. I have
taken no notice of your kind apologies. If I could

not be comfortable in your house, and with your family,
I should deserve to be miserable. If you could make
it convenient, I should wish to be with you by Monday
evening, as it would prevent the necessity of taking
fresh lodgings in town.

"With respectful compliments to Mrs. Gillman and
her sister, I remain, dear sir,

"Your much obliged,
"S. T. COLERIDGE."

This letter was written on a Saturday, and on the
Monday following Coleridge took up his residence
at Gillman's house.

The position was an extraordinary one. Coleridge's
life at this point had fallen to an extreme of insecurity
and dejection. He was now forty-four years of age,
and having no resources and no friends on whom he
could make further demands, separated from his
family, and being, as he always was, unable to assure for
himself any kind of settled income, he made this last
strange and desperate bid for protection, it may almost
be said, for life itself. The result was even more
remarkable. James Gillman's friendship for Coleridge
is one of the completely beautiful passages of literary
history. For eighteen years he received the poet in
his house, and attended to his health and comfort
with unwearying solicitude. Opium-taking as a habit
was cured, though it is not clear that Gillman did not
allow a very limited recourse to the drug at crises of
great pain. There was at first a formal pretence
of Coleridge making a small payment for his main-

tenance, but nothing permanent came of it, as may be imagined, and, in effect, Gillman, through all those years, took not a penny for his pains, and Coleridge was his welcome and honoured guest. The surgeon's kindness was unfailingly encouraged by his wife, and James and Ann Gillman not only became by far the most intimate friends of Coleridge's later life, but they redeemed those years with a domestic peace and relative freedom from anxiety such as he could otherwise have never known. It is greatly to the honour of both Coleridge and his two friends that there seems to have been between them no word that failed in courtesy and understanding from first to last. And the Gillmans were richly rewarded for their chivalry. Their house became one of the intellectual centres of England. There would meet Frederick Dennison Morris, Tennyson's Arthur Hallam, Basil Montagu, Hookham Frere, Julius Hare, John Wilson—the Christopher North of Blackwood's—and Wordsworth; here Carlisle and Emerson called, and here Charles Lamb was in the habit of coming for Sunday dinner. Gillman filled the part of host in this company with easy credit. His own claim to literary distinction seems to have consisted only of a prize won in his youth at the Royal College of Surgeons for a " Dissertation on the Bite of a Rabid Animal." But he was able to engage Coleridge in metaphysical talk by the hour, and come freshly out of the ordeal at the end, and that, as we all know, was no small achievement. Few men could survive an evening's dialectical contest with

Coleridge, but Gillman kept his end up for eighteen years.

It was while Coleridge was living at Highgate that the volume to which the following notes refer was given to him. It is Thomas Warton's edition of Milton's Shorter Poems. First published in 1785, this is the second edition, which appeared in 1791. Warton was the historian of English poetry, and Professor of Poetry at Oxford. He died in 1790, when Coleridge was eighteen. The book is inscribed, " To S. T. Coleridge, Esqre., with the love, regard, and esteem of his obliged and grateful friend J. Watson. Octr. 11th 1823." To this inscription is added another in Coleridge's writing, " I bequeath this Book to Mrs. Gillman. S. T. Coleridge, 28 June, 1827." And on a later leaf is yet a third, written in pencil, as follows:

" Presented to Robert Watson Cowen* by his aged friend Ann Gillman in remembrance of his much loved and highly esteemed Uncle John Watson, on whom the Almighty Giver of all good things had bestowed many precious gifts—early unaffected Piety, with a deep love of The True the Good, and the Beautiful. May 4th, 1854."

Ann Gillman was then seventy-five years of age, and lived six years longer. The John Watson here referred to is no doubt the original donor of the book.

* Mrs. Lucy E. Watson of Woburn Sands, Gillman's granddaughter, tells me that the John Watson referred to above was the son of a millowner at Dalston, near Carlisle, and the young friend to whom Coleridge paid some attention. This Watson was himself no family connection of the Gillmans. His sister was a Mrs. Cowen and Robert Watson Cowen was her son.

Coleridge, as was his habit, freely annotated the volume while he was reading it, and his notes, which have not hitherto been published, are here given with as little addition as possible.

The arrangement here adopted is as follows: The notes are numbered consecutively from one to forty-one. Each note is in two or three divisions—

(*a*) The extract from the text, or the editorial notes, of the edition of 1791, to which Coleridge's note refers, together with page reference.

(*b*) Coleridge's note.

(*c*) Any comment of my own where necessary. In a few instances these comments, for the sake of convenience, have been put elsewhere within square brackets.

*   *   *   *   *

On the fly-leaf of the volume:

" Of Criticism we may perhaps say, that these divine Poets, Homer, Eschylus, and the two Compeers, Dante, Shakespeare, Spencer, Milton, who deserve to have Critics, [   ] are placed above Criticism in the vulgar sense, and move in the sphere of Religion, while those who are not such, scarcely deserve Criticism, in any sense.—But speaking generally, it is far far better to distinguish Poetry into different Classes; and instead of fault-finding to say, this belongs to such or such a class—thus noting inferiority in the *sort* rather than censure on the particular poem or poet. We may *outgrow* certain *sorts* of poetry (Young's *Night-Thoughts*, for instance) without arraigning their excellence *proprio genere.* In short, the wise is the genial; and the genial judgement is to distinguish accurately the character and characteristics of each poem, praising them according to their force and vivacity in their own kind—and to reserve Reprehension for such as have no *character*—tho' the wisest reprehension would be not to speak of them at all."

*　　*　　*　　*　　*

1. *P. iii, Preface :*

A general note at the head of the Preface:

" Most shamefully incorrect. The Errata in the Latin Quotations are so numerous and so whimsical, as to puzzle the ingenuity of the best Latinist. I suspect that this is one of old Lackington's pirate editions. The paper seems too bad for such respectable Publishers, as the Robinsons, who did not deal in this [　　] *cactilis.*"

2. *P. iii, Preface :*

(*a*) Warton: " After the publication of the *Paradise Lost*, whose acknowledged merit and increasing celebrity. . ."

(*b*) Coleridge: " Can Tom Warton have been guilty of this offence against prose English ? ' Whose' instead of ' of which.' "

3. *P. iv, Preface :*

(*a*) Warton: " It was late in the present century, before they [Milton's early poems] attained their just measure of esteem and popularity. Wit and rhyme, sentiment and satire, polished numbers, sparkling couplets, and pointed periods, having so long kept undisturbed possession in our poetry, would not easily give way to fiction and fancy, to picturesque description, and romantic imagery."

(*b*) Coleridge: " It is hard to say which of the two kinds of metrical composition are here most unfaithfully characterized, that which Warton opposes to the Miltonic, or the Miltonic asserted to have been eclipsed by the former. But a marginal note does not give room enough to explain what I mean."

4. *P. xx, Preface :*

Coleridge's corrections—

> l. 10. re~~movit~~ " /novat."
> l. 15. Løn̨itur " /e /e."

5. *P.* 1, *Lycidas,* l. 1:

Yet once more, O ye laurels;

(*a*) Warton: " The best poets imperceptibly adopt phrases and formularies from the writings of their contemporaries or immediate predecessours. An Elegy on the death of the celebrated Countess of Pembroke, Sir Philip Sydney's sister, begins thus:

Yet once againe, my Muse."

(*b*) Coleridge: " This, no doubt, is true; but the application to particular instances is exceedingly suspicious. Why, in Heaven's name ! might not ' once more ' have as well occurred to Milton as to Sydney? On similar subjects or occasions some similar Thoughts *must* occur to different Persons, especially if men of resembling genius, quite independent of each other. The proof of this, if proof were needed, may be found in the works of contemporaries of different countries in books published at the very *same time,* where neither *could* have seen the work of the other—

perhaps ignorant of the language. I gave my lectures on Shakespear two years before Schlegel *began* his at Vienna, and I was myself startled at the close even verbal Parallelisms.—S. T. COLERIDGE."

6. *Pp.* 1-2, *Lycidas*, ll. 2-5:

> Ye myrtles brown, with ivy never sere,
> I come to pluck your berries harsh and crude;
> And with forc'd fingers rude,
> Shatter your leaves before the mellowing year:

(*a*) Warton: "Here is an inaccuracy of the poet. *The Mellowing Year* could not affect the leaves of the laurel, the myrtle and the ivy; which last is characterized before as *never sere*."

(*b*) Coleridge: "If this is not finding fault for fault-finding sake, Maister Tummas! I do not know what is. The young and diffident poet tells us, that the Duty to his Friend's memory compels him to produce a poem before his poetic Genius had attained its full development, or had received the due culture and nourishment from Learning and Study. The faculties appertaining to Poetic Genius he symbolizes beautifully and appropriately by the Laurel, the Myrtle and the Ivy—all three berry-bearing Plants: and these Berries express here the *actual* state, degree and quality of his poetic Powers, as the Plants themselves express the potential—the Leaves of the Ivy are 'never sere,' both because this is the general character of Ivy and of Verse, and by a natural and graceful Prolepsis in reference to his own future productions—now if Warton had *thought* instead of criticized, he must have seen that it was the Berries which were to be plucked, but that in consequence of their unripeness and the toughness of the pedicles he was in danger of *shattering* the Leaves in the attempt. It was the

Berries, I repeat, that the more advanced Season was to have *mellowed ;* and who indeed ever dreamt of *mellowing* a Leaf ? ! The autumn may be said to mellow the *tints* of the Foliage; but the word is never applied to the Leaves themselves.—S. T. C."

7. *P.* 3, *Lycidas*, ll. 10-11:

> He knew
> Himself to sing, and build the lofty rhime.

(*a*) Warton in a note says that the lofty rhime means " lofty verse," as in

> Things unattempted yet in prose or rhyme.

and adds—

" I cannot, however, admit bishop Pearce's reasoning, who says: ' Milton appears to have meant a different thing by Rhime here from Rime in his Preface, where it is six times mentioned, and always spelled without an *h :* whereas in all the Editions, Rhime in this place of the poem was spelled with an *h*. Milton probably meant a difference in the thing, by making so constant a difference in the spelling; and intended we should here understand by Rhime not the *jingling sound of like Endings, but Verse in general.*' "

(*b*) Coleridge: " I am still inclined to think Bishop Pearce in the right. It is the tendency of all Languages to avail them of the opportunities given by accidental differences of pronunciation and spelling to make a word multiply on itself: *ex-gr.*, Propriety, Property; Mister and Master.—Besides, we can prove that this was Milton's plan. In the First Edition of the Par. Lost in *Twelve* Books, called the Second Edition, Heè, Sheè, are systematically thus distinguished from He, and She; and her, their from hir, thir—when they are to convey a distinct image to the mind, and are not merely grammatical adjuncts, such as would be *understood* in Latin."

8. *Pp.* 4-5, *Lycidas*, ll. 15, 18:

> Begin then, Sisters of the sacred well,
>
> *   *   *   *   *
>
> Hence with denial vain, and coy excuse:

(*a*) Warton: "The epithet, Coy is at present restrained to Person. Antiently, it was more generally combined. Thus a shepherd in Drayton's Pastorals—

> Shepherd, these things are all TOO COY for me,
> Whose youth is spent in jollity and mirth.

That is, 'This sort of knowledge is too *hard*, too difficult for me,' etc."

(*b*) Coleridge: "Why, Warton! dear Tom Warton! wake up, my good fellow! You are snoring. Even in Drayton's Pastoral the 'coy' is poorly explained into 'hard'; but here it is evidently *personal*—excuse showing coyness in the Sisters."

9. *P.* 5, *Lycidas*, ll. 23-26:

> For we were nurst upon the self-same hill,
> Fed the same flock by fountain, shade, and rill.
> Together both, ere the high lawns appear'd
> Under the opening eye-lids of the morn,

(*a*) Warton: "Here a new paragraph begins in the edition of 1645, and in all that followed. But in the edition of 1638, the whole context is thus pointed and arranged" [As above].

(*b*) Coleridge: "It is astonishing to me, that Warton should not have felt that the couplet

> For we were nurst upon the self-same Hill,
> Fed the same flock by fountain, shade, and rill !

is manifestly the Base or Pedestal of the Stanza or scheme of verse, commencing with, ' Begin then, Sisters,' and that it is divided from the eighth line of the Scheme by a colon: *i.e.* a full stop intended but with the cadence revoked, as it were, by a sudden recollection of some appertaining matter, confirming, enforcing or completing the preceding thought.   Then follows a Pause, during which the Thought last started and expressed generally, unfolds itself to the poet's mind—and he begins anew with the proof and exposition of it by the particulars.—Another, and for a poet's ear convincing, proof that the couplet belongs to the third stanza is, that the eighth line like the first is rhymeless and was left so, because the concurring rhymes of the concluding Distich were foreseen as the compensations. Mem. This applicable to Sonnets, viz. under what circumstances the Sonnet should be 8+6, 12+2 or 14.

" But this is nothing to the want of Tact, Taste, and Ear—yea, of Eye and sagacious nostril—in the evidenced preference given to the Edit. 1638.—The Sstt [?Stanza] begins anew with, Together, etc. After shroud there should be a colon only."

10. *P.* 8, *Lycidas*, ll. 37-44:

> But, O the heavy change, now thou art gone,
> Now thou art gone, and never must return !
> Thee, Shepherd, thee the woods, and desert caves
> With wild thyme and the gadding vine o'ergrown,
> And all their echoes mourn:
> The willows, and the hazel copses green,
> Shall now no more be seen
> Fanning their joyous leaves to thy soft lays.

(*b*) Coleridge: " There is a delicate beauty of sound produced by the floating or oscillation of Assonance and Consonance, in the rhymes gone, return, caves, o'ergrown, mourn, green, seen, lays. Substitute 'flown' for 'gone' in the first line: and if you have a Poet's ear, you will feel what you have lost and understand what I mean. I am bound, however, to confess that in the five last lines of this Stanza I find more of the fondness of a classical scholar for his favourite Classics than of the self-subsistency of a Poet destined to be himself a Classic,—more of the Copyist of Theocritus and *his* Copyist, Virgil than of the free Imitator, who seizes with a strong hand whatever he wants or wishes for his own purpose and justifies the seizure by the improvement of the material or the superiority of the purpose, to which it is applied."

(*c*) The lines referred to presumably follow those quoted; Coleridge is a little pernikety here.

11. *P. 11, Lycidas*, ll. 56-57:

> Ay me! I fondly dream!
> Had ye been there for what could that have done?

(*a*) Warton prints these lines as above, and appends the following note: " So these lines stand in editions 1638, 1645, and 1673, the two last of which were printed under Milton's eye. Doctor Newton thus exhibits the passage:

> Ay me! I fondly dream
> Had ye been there, for what could that have done?

and adds this note: 'We have here followed the pointing of Milton's manuscript in preference to all the editions: and the meaning plainly is, I fondly *dream of your having been there*, for what would that have signified?' But surely the words, *I fondly dream had ye been there*, will not bear this construction. The reading which I have adopted, to say nothing of its authority, has an abruptness which heightens the present sentiment, and more strongly marks the distraction of the speaker's mind. ' Ah me ! I am fondly dreaming ! I will suppose you had been there—*but why should I suppose it*, for what would that have availed ?' The context is broken and confused, and contains a sudden elliepsis which I have supplied with the words in Italics."

(*b*) Coleridge: "Had this been Milton's intention, he would have written *but*, as W. has done; and not for. Newton's is clearly the true Reading."

12. *P.* 13, *Lycidas*, l. 63:

> Down the swift Hebrus to the Lesbian shore ?

(*a*) Warton tells us in a note that Milton was misled by Virgil in the use of the epithet *swift*, and quotes Servius in reproof of Virgil.

(*b*) Coleridge: " ' Smooth ' would have suited M.'s purpose even better than ' swift,' even tho' the latter had not been inappropriate, as poetically contrasting with the vehemence and turbulence of the preceding Lines.—Possibly, Milton was at this period of his life too predominantly a Poet to have read Servius. Mem. The Virgilian Line might not unhappily be applied to the Hon. Mr. B****., who has made a more hasty ' Cut and run ' than his *past* friend, H—r—. ' Volucremque fuga prævertitur Hebrum,' *i.e.*

> Prick't from behind by Fear, his Legs his Bail,
> Outruns swift HEBER following at his *Tail*."

13. *P.* 44, *L'Allegro*, ll. 23-24:

> Fill'd her with thee a daughter fair,
> So buxum, blithe, and debonair.

(*a*) Warton says that somebody else is of opinion that this passage was based on lines from *Pericles Prince of Tyre*.

(*b*) Coleridge: " Perhaps no more convincing proof can be given that the power of poetry is from a *Genius*, *i.e.* not included in the faculties of the human mind common to all men, than these so frequent ' opinions,' that this and that passage was formed from, or borrowed, or stolen, etc., from this or that other passage, found in some other poet or poem, three or three hundred years older. In the name of common sense, if Gower could write the lines without having seen Milton, why not Milton have done so tho' Gower had never existed ? That Mr. Bowle or Bishop Newton, or Mr. Cory, etc., should be unable to imagine the origination of a fine thought, is no way strange; but that *Warton* should fall into the same dull cant— ! !"

(*c*) The Gower referred to by Warton is the Gower in Shakespeare's play, not Moral Gower the poet.

14. *P. 64, L'Allegro,* ll. 133-134:

> Or sweetest Shakespeare, Fancy's child,
> Warble his native wood-notes wild.

(*a*) Warton quotes Bishop Hurd's note: " Milton shows his judgement here, in celebrating Shakespeare's *Comedies*, rather than his Tragedies. For models of the latter, he refers us rightly, in his PENSEROSO, to the Grecian scene, V. 97."

(*b*) Coleridge: " H. thou Right Reverend Aspirate ! what hadst thou to do with sweetest Shakespeare ? Was it not enough to *merder* the Prophets ? But to be serious—if by Tragedies Hurd means *Songs of the Goat*, and if there were any Pagans that had to make such, they would have to look to the Ancient Greeks for Models. But what Shakespear proposed to realise was—an Imitation of human actions in connection with sentiments, passions, characters, incidents, and events for the purpose of pleasureable emotion; so that whether this be shown by Tears of Laughter or Tears of Tenderness, they shall still be Tears of Delight, and united with intellectual complacency. Call such a work a Drama: and then I will tell the whole Herd of Hurdite Critics, that the Dramas of Shakespear, whether the lighter or the loftier emotions preponderate, are all, the one no less than the others, *Models*, with which it would be cruel and most unjust to the Manes either of Eschylus, Sophocles, Euripides, or of Aristophanes to compare the *Tragedies* of the former or the Comedies of the latter. Shakespere produced Dramatic Poems, not Tragedies nor Comedies. . . . If the Greek Tragedies, or as H. affectedly expresses it, ' The Greek Scene ' be a Model for anything modern, it must be for the Opera houses.—S. T. C."

15. *Pp*. 67-76, *Il. Penseroso*, ll. 1-60:

(*b*) Coleridge: " The first sixty lines are (with unfeigned diffidence I add) in my humble ~~opinion~~ judgement not only inferior to the *Allegro*, but such as many a secondrate Poet, & Pygmy compared with Milton might have written."

16. *Pp*. 88-89, *Il. Penseroso*, ll. 146-150:

> Entice the dewy-feather'd sleep;
> And let some strange mysterious dream
> Wave at his wings in aery stream
> Of lively portraiture display'd,
> Softly on my eye-lids laid.

(*a*) Warton: " I do not exactly understand the whole of the context. Is the Dream to wave at Sleep's wings? Doctor Newton will have *wave* to be a verb

neuter: and very justly, as the passage now stands.
But let us strike out *at*, and make *wave* active.

> —Let some mysterious dream
> Wave his wings, in airy stream, etc.

' Let some fantastic DREAM put the wings of SLEEP in
motion, which shall be *displayed*, or expanded, in an
airy or soft *stream* of visionary imagery, gently falling
or settling on my eye-lids.' Or, *his* may refer to DREAM,
and not to SLEEP, with much the same sense. In the
meantime, supposing *lively* adverbial, as was now
common, *displayed* will connect with *pourtraiture*,
that is, ' pourtraiture lively displayed,' with this sense,
' Wave his wings, in an airy stream of rich pictures so
strongly displayed in vision as to resemble real *Life*.'
Or, if *lively* remain an adjective, much in the same
sense, *displayed* will signify *displaying* itself. On
the whole, we must not here seek for precise meanings
of parts, but acquiesce in a general idea resulting from
the whole, which I think is sufficiently seen."

(*b*) Coleridge: " A winged Dream upon a winged
Sleep on the Poet's eye-lids ! More Sacks on the Mill !
Warton must have written these notes in a careless
hurry."

" Explain the four lines as you will, and tinker them as
how you can, they will remain a confused and awkwardly
arranged period. But the *construing* I take to be this—
and at his wings (dewy-feather'd) softly laid on my
eyelids let some strange Dream flow waveringly in aery
stream of lively portraiture—*display'd* being a rhyme
to ' laid,' and therefore not *quite* superfluous.—S. T. C.
P.S. If any conjectural Reading were admissible,
I should prefer

> Weave on his wings its aery scheme (or theme)
> In lively, etc."

17. *P. 93, Il Penseroso :*

(*a*) At the end of *Il Penseroso* Warton quotes Hurd's note: " Of these two exquisite little poems, [*L'Allegro* and *Il Penseroso*] I think it clear that this last is the most taking; which is owing to the subject. The mind delights most in these solemn images, and a genius delights most to pain them."

(*b*) Coleridge: " I feel the direct opposite, almost painfully. But I suspect, that this contrariety would go thro' all my decisions in reference to Bishop Hurd's."

18. *P.* 152, *Comus*, l. 108:

And Advice with scrupulous head.

(*a*) " The manuscript reading, *And quick Law*, is the best. It is not the essential attribute of *Advice* to be *Scrupulous:* but it is of *Quick Law*, or *Watchful Law*, to be so."

[This is a note of Warburton's quoted by Warton. A fact which Coleridge overlooks in his note which follows.]

(*b*) Coleridge: " Bless me ! Who would have expected a remark so tasteless or so shallow a reason from Warton ? It is not the essential character of Advice, but it is the very character, by which the God of Riot and Wassail would ridicule him. And then the sound and rhythm. *Quick* law and the confusion of executive (Quick) with judicial Law, (Scrupulous). In short the wonder is that it should be found in the manuscript as having occurred to Milton."

19. P. 155, *Comus*, l. 140:

From her cabin'd loop-hole peep,

(*a*) At line 140, Warton, in a cross reference to *Paradise Lost* refers to Milton's use of the loop-holes in the Indian fig-tree in Book IX. He adds: " Milton was a student in botany. He took his description of this multifarious tree from the account of it in Gerard's HERBALL,"—an account that Warton quotes.

(*b*) Coleridge: " If I wished to display the charm and *effect* of metre and the *art* of poetry, independent of the Thoughts and Images—the superiority, in short of *poematic* over *prose* Composition, the poetry or no-poetry being the same in both, I question, whether a more apt and convincing instance could be found, than in these exquisite lines of Milton's compared with the passage in Gerald [sic], of which they are the organized version. Shakespeare's Cleopatra on the Cydnus, compared with the original in North's Plutarch is another almost equally striking example.—S. T. C. 22nd Oct^r., 1823. Ramsgate."

20. *P.* 168, *Comus*, ll. 238-239:

O, if thou have
Hid them in some flow'ry cave,

(*a*) Warton: " Here is a seeming inaccuracy for the sake of the rhyme. But the sense being hypothetical and contingent, we will suppose an elleipsis of *shouldest* before *have*."

(*b*) Coleridge: " Could W. have been so ignorant of English Grammar ? His Brother would have flogged a Winchester Lad for an equivalent ignorance in a Latin Subjunctive."

(*c*) Thomas Warton's brother was Joseph Warton, himself a poet and critic of distinction, and according to the *National Dictionary of Biography* " the con-spicuously unsuccessful Headmaster " of Winchester from 1766 to 1793.

21. *P.* 188, *Comus,* l. 380:

> Were all to ruffled, and sometimes impair'd.

(*a*) Warton: " ALL-TO or AL-TO, is *Intirely.*"

(*b*) Coleridge: " Even this is not the exact meaning of to—or all-to which answers to the German *Zer,* as our *for* in forlorn to ver, pronounced fer."

22. *Pp.* 241-242, *Comus,* ll. 892-895:

> My sliding chariot stays,
> Thick set with agat, and the azurn sheen
> Of turkis blue, and emrald green,
> That in the channel strays;

(*b*) Coleridge: " L. 895. The word ' strays ' *neëded* a Note—and therefore it is the only part of the sentence left unnoticed.   First of all, Turquoises and Emeralds are not much addicted to *straying* anywhere; and the last place, I should look for them, would be in channels; and secondly, the verb is in the singular number and belongs to Sheen, *i.e.* Lustre, Shininess, as its nominative case.   It may therefore bear a question, whether Milton did mean the wandering flitting tints and hues of the Water, in my opinion a more poetical as well as a much more appropriate Imagery.   He particularizes one precious stone, the Agate, which often occurs in brooks and rivulets, and leaves the *substance* of the other ornaments as he had of the chariot itself undetermined, and describes them by the effect on the eye/thickset with agate and that transparent, or humid, shine of (turquoise-like) Blue, and (emeraldine) Green that strays in the channel.   For it is in the water immediately above the pebbly Bed of the Brook, that one seems to see these lovely glancing Water-tints. *N.B.*—This note in the best style of Warburtonian perverted ingenuity."

(*c*) The jape of Coleridge's is at himself, since the notes on this passage are Warton's and not quoted from Warburton.

23. *P.* 250, *Comus*, ll. 946-956:

> And not many furlongs thence
> Is your Father's residence,
> Where this night are met in state
> Many a friend to gratulate
> His wish'd presence, and beside
> All the swains that near abide,
> With jigs, and rural dance resort;
> We shall catch them at their sport,
> And our sudden coming there
> Will double all their mirth and chear.

(*b*) Coleridge: " With all prostration of reverence at the feet of even the Juvenal, Milton, I must yet lift up my head enough to pillow my chin on the Rose of his Shoe, and ask him in a timid whisper whether Rhymes and Finger-metre do not render poor flat prose ludicrous, rather than tend to elevate it, or even to hide its nakedness."

24. *P.* 272, *Ode on the Morning of Christ's Nativity*, l. 116:

> With unexpressive notes. . . .

(*b*) Coleridge: " It is strange that *Milton* should have held it allowable to substitute the active Aorist *ive* for the passive adjectivable. It was too high a compliment even to Shakespear.

" What should we think of ' undescriptive ' for ' indescribable '? Surely, no authority can justify such a solecism."

25. *P.* 274, *Ode on the Morning of Christ's Nativity,*
Stanza XV. :

> Yea Truth and Justice then
> Will down return to men,
>   Orb'd in a rainbow; and like glories wearing
> Mercy will sit between,
> Thron'd in celestial sheen,
>   With radiant feet the tissued clouds down steering:
> And heav'n, as at some festival,
> Will open wide the gate of her high palace hall.

(*b*) Coleridge: " XV. A glorious subject for the
Ceiling of a princely Banquet-room, in the style of
Parmeggiano or Allston.—S. T. C."

"Stanza XXIII. I think I have seen—possibly
Fuseli."

26. *P.* 281, *On the Morning of Christ's Nativity,*
ll. 229-231:

> So when the sun in bed,
> Curtain'd with cloudy red,
>   Pillows his chin upon an orient wave. . . .

(*a*) Warton: " The words *pillows* and *chin*, throw
an air of burlesque and familiarity over a comparison
most exquisitely conceived and adapted."

(*b*) Coleridge: " I have tried in vain to imagine,
in what other way the Image could be given.   I rather
think that it is one of the Hardinesses permitted to a
great Poet. Dante would have written it: tho' it is
most in the spirit of Donne."

27. *P.* 286, *The Passion :*

This poem breaks off at the end of Stanza VIII.,
and Milton subjoins the following note:

" This subject, the Author finding to be above the years he had, when he wrote it, and nothing satisfied with what was begun, left it unfinished."

(*b*) Coleridge: "I feel grateful to Milton that instead of preserving only the VIth and the first five lines of the VIIIth stanza, he has given us the whole eight. The true solution of 1st, 2nd, 3rd, 4th, vth and 7th stanzas is, that Milton had not yet *un*taught himself the looking up to inferior minds, which he had been taught to consider as Models. He did not yet dare to know, how great he was."

28. *P.* 307, *At a Vacation Exercise*, ll. 3-6:

> And mad'st imperfect words with childish trips,
> Half unpronounc'd, slide through my infant-lips,*
> Driving dumb silence from the portal door,
> Where he had mutely sat two years before.†

(*b*) Coleridge: " ' *Slide ' seems to me not quite the right word. Perhaps ' stumble ' or ' struggle ' would be better ? Omitting ' my.'

> Half unpronounced, stumbles thro' infant lips."

†" Well might He speak late who spoke to such purpose !"

29. *P.* 312, *At a Vacation Exercise*, l. 60:

> The faery ladies danc'd upon the hearth. . . .

(*a*) Warton has a note saying that fairies and Aristotle's ten categories were both in fashion and both exploded at the same time.

(*b*) Coleridge: "Exploded ? The Categories ? Aristotle's *Table* of the Categories was corrected and improved, but even this not till long after the Date of this Exercise."

30. *P.* 314, *At a Vacation Exercise*, l. 83:

> To find a foe it shall not be his hap. . . .

(*a*) Warton: " *Substantia, substantiae nova contrariatur,* is a school maxim."

(*b*) Coleridge: " It is curious that on this purely logical conception, or rather *form* of conceiving, Spinoza re-codified the Pantheism of the old Greek philosophy.—S. T. C."

31. *Pp.* 318-319, *On the University Carrier* (Two poems):

(*a*) Warton quotes Hurd's note on Milton's two pieces on Hobson, the University Carrier: " I wonder Milton should suffer these two things on Hobson to appear in his edition of 1645. He, who at the age of nineteen, had so just a contempt for,

> Those new-fangled toys, and trimming flight,
> Which take our new fantastics with delight."

(*b*) Coleridge: " It is truly edifying to observe, what value and importance certain Critics attach to a farthing's worth of paper. One *wonders*—another *regrets*—just as if the two poor copies of verses had been a Dry-rot, threatening the whole life and beauty of Comus, Lycidas, and other work in their vicinity! I confess that I have read these *Hobsons* 20 times, and always with amusement, without the least injury to the higher and very different Delight afforded by Milton's *poetry.*—These are the Junior Soph's very learned Jocularitys.—S. T. C."

" And why should not Milton as well as other Cantabs like to chuckle over his old College Jokes and crack them anew."

32. *P.* 330, *Sonnet IV.*, ll. 1-2:

> Diodati, e te'l dirò con maraviglia,
>   Quel ritroso io ch'ampor spreggiar foléa. . . .

(*b*) Coleridge's corrections:

ma/raviglia   e/
ch'~~ampor~~   ch'amor

33. *P.* 340, *Sonnet to Mr. H. Lawes :*

(*b*) Coleridge: " It is rather singular that the compliment to a musician by the most musical of all poets and who loved the man as well as his Art, should be the least musical of all the Sonnets—notwithstanding the sweetness of the last 3 lines.—S. T. C."

34. *P.* 376, *Translation of Psalm VII. :*

(*a*) Warton comments on this poem: " This is a very pleasing stanza, and which I do not elsewhere recollect."

(*b*) Coleridge: " A B A B B A. A more pleasing stanza might I think be constructed for a *shorter* poem by extending it to eight lines

A B A B B A B A

ire rage fire cage page sire wage lyre."

35. *P.* 379, *Translation of Psalm VIII. Second Stanza :*

> Out of the mouths of babes and sucklings thou
>   Hast founded strength because of all thy foes,
> To stint th'enemy, and slack th'avenger's brow,
>   That bends his rage thy providence t'oppose.

(*b*) Coleridge: " A truly majestic composition. Milton pronounced Jē hŏ vāh, as an amphimacer.—S. T. C."

"Milton's ear taught him that accent even with emphasis, provided the latter be slight, quickens the sound. I doubt not, that Milton meant that there should be no elision of the e final of the definite article, but intended thĕ ĕnĕmў for a dicretic or tetrabrach isochronous only to an emphasized Iambic. I find it easy to read the line so as to give it a good and striking metrical effect, by at once rapidly and yet emphatically pronouncing ' the ènemy ' with a smart stroke on the ' en.'—S. T. COLERIDGE."

36. *P.* 379, *Translation of Psalm VIII. Fifth Stanza,* ll. 1-2:

> O'er the works of thy hand thou mad'st him Lord,
> Thou hast put all under his lordly feet. . . .

(*b*) Coleridge: " The two first lines of the 5th stanza are more difficult. Yet even here there needs only an educated ear. In the first line the two last feet properly read are almost spondees instead of iambics: the others, a trochee and a choriambic. Now count the four last syllables as equal to six breves, and you have the same number of times as in pure Iambics, and the spondaic character of the two last feet compensating for the quickened utterance of the 3 former."

37. *Pp.* 385-386, *Translation of Psalm LXXXII. :*

(*b*) Coleridge: " With a few alterations this Psalm might be adopted in a new church version, or at least a revision of Sternhold."

38. *P.* 386, *Translation of Psalm LXXXII.,* l. 24:

> As other Princes *die.*

(*b*) Coleridge: " Other ? Ought not the word to

have been in italics? This is the only passage or verse in the Old Testament in which I can imagine any allusion to the fall of the Spirits, the Thrones, or Potentates. Our Lord plainly interpreted the verse in this sense."

39. *P.* 421, *Latin Elegy to Charles Deodate,* 1. 12:

> Nec dudum vetiti me laris angit amor.

(*a*) Warton reads this passage as showing "that Milton was sentenced to undergo a temporary removal or rustication from Cambridge."

(*b*) Coleridge: "I cannot agree with Warton. It seems to me far more probable that Deodate, in a pedantic fit had called Milton's vacation an exile from the Muses—and that Milton tacitly, or rather implicitly, reproves his friend's pedantry. But how Warton could have so utterly mistaken the sense of the eleven and twelve lines is astonishing!"

40. *P.* 429, *Latin Elegy to Charles Deodate,* 1. 7:

> Jactet, et Ausoniis plena theatra stolis.

(*b*) Coleridge: "Remarkable, that a man of so fine an ear as Milton, should have endured a short syllable before *St.* theatra *stolis.*"

41. *P.* 533, *Sylvarum Liber,* 1. 6:

> Adesdum, et haec s'is verba pauca Salsillo

(*b*) Coleridge's correction

> *haec*   hanc ?

COLERIDGE'S "ZAPOLYA"

COLERIDGE'S "ZAPOLYA"

ZAPOLYA, Coleridge's essay "in humble imitation of The Winter's Tale" as he calls it, was published by Rest Fenner in 1817. There had previously been negotiations with Murray, which fell through after the play had been declined for production by Drury Lane,* in circumstances of which Coleridge writes at length to Murray in his letter of February 27, 1817.†

The play is one of the many written by English poets at periods when poets were not wanted in the theatre. It belongs to a date long after Coleridge's time of mighty inspiration, but it makes no bad company for the fireside if taken up and read, as the poet desired, "as a Christmas tale." It was composed when imaginative drama was exiled from the theatre, and with the inevitable result. It could hardly succeed on the stage.

Zapolya was reprinted in the collected editions of 1828, 1829, 1834; and many subsequent dates, up to Mr. E. H. Coleridge's definitive edition of 1912.

---

* After the successful publication of the play, a "version" of it was produced at the Surrey Theatre. [See Thomas J. Wise's *Bibliography of Coleridge* (1913), p. 111.]

† *Letters of Samuel Taylor Coleridge*, edited by Ernest Hartley Coleridge, 1895, vol. ii., p. 665 *seq.* Heinemann.

Various textual alterations were introduced after the
first edition of 1817, but those now noted have not
been used. They are in Coleridge's writing, partly
marginal, partly embodied in the printed text. Though
not important, they make for a nicer dramatic propriety, in letting Glycine tell of Bethlen's angry
moods instead of giving the speech to Bethlen himself;
and the alternative images of the island are of interest.

Coleridge seems hardly to have been able to keep
his pen away from any book (his own or another's)
that came into his hands. It is known that this was
not the only copy of *Zapolya* that he adorned with his
own alterations: in the present case the failure to have
used them in later editions may have been deliberate;
it is at least as likely that he forgot all about them.

The text of pages 54 and 56 of Act I., Scene I., in the
first edition of *Zapolya*, 1817, from " Blest spirit of
my parents " to " was a widow's mantle," runs thus:

BETH: Blest spirit of my parents,
       Ye hover o'er me now ! Ye shine upon me !
       And, like a flower that coils forth from a Ruin,
       I feel and seek the light, I can not see !
SAROL: Thou see'st yon dim spot on the mountain's ridge,
       But what it is thou know'st not. Even such
       Is all I know of thee—haply, brave youth,
       Is all, Fate makes it safe for thee to know :
BETH: Safe ? Safe ? O let me then inherit danger,
       And it shall be my birth-right:
SAROL (*aside*):   That look again.
       The wood which first encloses, and then skirts
       The highest track that leads across the mountains—
       Thou know'st it, Bethlen ?

BETH: Lady, 'twas my wont
To roam there in my childhood oft alone
And mutter to myself the name of father.
For still Bathory (why, till now I guess'd not)
Would never hear it from my lips, but sighing
Gaz'd upward.   Yet of late an idle terror—

GLY: Madam, that wood is haunted by the war-wolves,
Vampires, and monstrous—

SAROL: (*with a smile*):   Moon-calves, credulous girl!
Haply some o'ergrown savage of the forest
Hath his lair there, and fear hath framed the rest.
                    Then speaking again to Bethlen.
After that last great battle (O young man!
Thou wakest anew my life's sole anguish), that
Which fixed Lord Emerick on his throne, Bathory
Led by a cry, far inward from the track,
In the hollow of an oak, as in a nest,
Did find thee, Bethlen, then an helpless babe.
The robe that wrapt thee, was a widow's mantle.

The amended text as altered by Coleridge in the copy
before me is as follows:

BETH: Blest spirit of my parents,
Ye hover o'er me now!   Ye shine upon me!
And, like a flower that coils from forth a Ruin,
I feel and seek the light, I can not see!
O tell me all!

SAROL: A poor imperfect Tale,
Dim as the Relique of a moulder'd Roll,
Is all I know of thee—haply, brave youth,
Is all, Fate makes it safe for thee to know!

BETH: Safe?   Safe?   O let me then inherit danger,
And it shall be my birth-right!
                                    Yon black Line—

SAROL :

GLY: The Forest, where, they say, the War-wolf haunts
Vampires and monstrous—

SAROL: Moon-calves, credulous Girl:
         Thou know'st it, Bethlen ?
GLY: Well he knows it, Lady !
         For he has told me how while yet a child,
         Oft in his moods, when anger'd at Bathory,
         Because he would not let me say, My Father,
         He'd wander there, on purpose to alarm him,
         Muttring or shouting the forbidden sound
         Along the track, that leads across the Mountain.
SAROL: Led by a cry, far inward from that track,
         In the hollow of an oak, as in a nest,
         Did find thee, Bethlen, then an helpless babe.
         The robe, that wrapt thee, was a widow's mantle.

On p. 57, Bethlen's speech at the top of the page

         And did he leave her ?   What had I a mother ?
         And left her bleeding, dying ?   Bought I vile life
         With the desertion of a dying mother ?
         O agony !

is altered by Coleridge to

         And did he leave her ?   Was this vile life bought
         With the desertion of a dying mother ?
         O agony !

Sarolta's speech below, which in the printed text
runs

                               Hush, Glycine !
         It is the ground-swell of a teeming instinct:
         Let it but lift itself to air and sunshine,
         And it will find a mirror in the waters,
         It now makes boil above it.   Check him not !

is extended in Coleridge's notes thus:

> Hush, Glycine!
> It is the ground-swell of a teeming instinct:
> Or like an Isle forced up by nether fires—
> Let it but lift itself to air and sunshine,
> And it will find a mirror in the waters,
> It now makes boil above it.   Check him not!

Coleridge, moreover, on the page has made the following trials for the added line:

> A sea-born Isle forced up by nether fires—

> Like to some island Mass from Ocean's Bed
> Unloosed, and shoulder'd up by nether fires,

> By nether fires unloos'd, and struggling upward.

LANDOR'S " DRY STICKS FAGOTED "

LANDOR'S "DRY STICKS FAGOTED"

*D*RY STICKS FAGOTED, by Walter Savage Landor, was published in 1858 with the following imprint, *Edinburgh : James Nichol*, 104, *High Street, London : James Nisbet and Co.* I have before me a series of thirty-eight letters and notes written by Landor to Nichol with reference to the book while it was going through the press. These are almost all undated, with no more than here and there a " Saturday night " or " Monday morning," and twice a date, " Oct. 14 " with no year, and " October 23, '57," and they deal largely with matters of unimportant detail. But they have several points of interest, of which the following is a summary. I have numbered the letters 1 to 38, in the order in which they were written so far as I can determine this from internal evidence. I have enclosed my own notes in square brackets.

1. " Saturday Night. I find that I sent one poem to you this morning which is in the *Last Fruits.*"

[This is characteristic of the confusion in which Landor always seems to have been with his manuscripts. More than once in preparing *Dry Sticks Fagoted* for the press he found himself including poems that had already been printed in *The Last Fruit Off an Old Tree*. 1853.]

2. "There are a few pieces should [which] I must try to collect back from my friends—not having a copy."

3. "In the 160 pages of the poems sent to me, I do not find ' My little kid.' "

[The poem *To a Kid* is No. 287, of D.S.F., p. 167. See later references.]

4. "I have been looking in vain for a short one, beginning ' My little kid! if I forbid.' It would grieve me to lose it. . . . I do trust that you will have no occasion to prove your kindness in looking long for duplicates in the *Last Fruits*. . . . The *Little Kid* was in some periodical, a year or two ago."

5. "The Little Kid is not among the poems in The Last Fruits. It was certainly sent and I think printed in this edition. Mr. Linton sent it to me, and I can get no other copy, nor remember where it first appeared."

6. "Saturday Morning. My niece was with me when I received, thro' Mr. Linton, the *Little Kid*, and congratulated me on recovering it. She was also with me when I received and returned the proof. So, beyond a doubt, this poet was cast aside among those cancelled. Probably one or two more shared the same fate. It was not in the Last Fruits."

7. "Saturday Evening. A lady, after some days, has found and sent to me the *Little Kid*. Here it is."

8. " In my great hurry for the post this morning,
I forgot that I omitted the heading to *Mother Pest-
come*. It is, The pilfered to the pilferer."

[This is one of the poems that led to Landor's
prosecution by the Rev. Morris Yescombe and his wife.
Landor had to pay a thousand pounds damages.
No. 125, D.S.F., p. 70.]

9. " Sunday Night. Here is a line which I request
you to substitute in those verses on myself, to which
there is a line of notes."

[This refers to *Sermoni Propiora*, No. 207, D.S.F.,
p. 113. The seventh line originally ran,

Southey and Hare and Hamilton and Ward. . . .

This was in the manuscript of the poem, which is also
before me, and also in the first proof. A note refers
Hamilton and Ward to Sir William Hamilton and
Lord Dudley. In Letter 9 Landor alters the line to

Drummond and Gell, the triad Hares, and Ward,

with notes referring the triad Hares to Francis,
Augustus and Julius, and Ward again to Lord Dudley.
In the second proof the line is altered to,

Drummond and Hare and wise and witty Ward,

the Lord Dudley note still standing. In the third
proof it becomes,

Gell, Drummond, Hare, and wise and witty Ward,

the note now referring to Lord Dudley and Ward.
This is how the line stands in the published book.]

10. "The following verse must be added to the *Heroics*, ending now with Letterman Graham, And (removed over the way) the old slopshop of Ben-Disraeli."

[This refers to *Heroics or Dactylics*, No. 106, D.F.S., p. 62. The line was not, however, added.]

11. [Nothing to be noted.]

12. "I have no Athenaeums or Frazers. I am confident that *several* of my poems are in both, of the 3 or 4 years past.

"The printer is incorrigible. In p. 50 I corrected a word he would retain—never having heard of quail. Now there are some which may serve for substitutes, I would erase what must, and perhaps should, be unintelligible to most readers, if not to all—for instance that in p. 109. There is another 228 on p. 128 which must also be erased."

[The references are:

(*a*) *The Pacific Hero*, No. 87, D.S.F., p. 50.

> And Earth shall quail before his baton.

In three proofs the printer, in spite of corrections, put "quell" instead of "quail."

(*b*) No. 197, D.S.F., p. 109, is *Hypocrisy why Hated*. In the original proof it was a poem called *Preferences*, which ran as follows:

> It may be true as you declare
> That very few on earth there are
> Whom you prefer to me.

> Obliged to take for it your word,
> Take mine; I'd rather you prefer'd
> The universe than X.

In the second proof this was erased, and in the third proof the present poem was substituted.

(c) No. 228, D.S.F., p. 128, is *Ignorance of Botany*. In the first proof it was *One Indifferent to Animals*, as follows:

> For animals, half beast or wholly,
> How very little do you feel!
> Pity the bandy legs of Folly;
> And lift the turnspit to his wheal.

In the second proof this is erased, and in the third the present poem substituted.

The cancelled poems do not seem to have been printed elsewhere.]

13. "*The Achilles and Helen*—must, I think, be either in the Athenaeum or Frazers Magazine, or the Daily Advertiser, sent last year."

[*Achilles and Helena on Ida* is No. 314, D.S.F., p. 180. See later references.]

14. "Wednesday Morning. Mr. Linton has been looking for the 'Achilles and Helen' which he thinks *must* be Frazer or the Athenaeum.—But there is some other Scotch Editor of a Magazine in London (*not* Blackwood) to whom my friends may possibly have sent it. Mr. Linton asks me whether I sent to you the *Plaint of Freedom*. I do not know. I trust some diligent enquirer will find the Achilles."

[Lines *To the Author of " The Plaint of Freedom"* are No. 241, D.S.F., p. 135. *The Plaint of Freedom* was a volume of poems by W. J. Linton, published in 1852, and it was dedicated " To the Memory of Milton."]

15. " I shall be in state of trepidation until I see proofs of these. I do trust the Helen will be found yet. Certainly it must be in Frazer or the Athenaeum —tho' perhaps five or six years back."

16. " I must now make one final effort to recover my Achilles and Helen. Nothing I ever wrote is comparable to this poem; and it would bitterly grieve me if your volume should appear without it. My memory is almost gone: names, dates, places, I never can recollect. . . . The *Plaint of Freedom*, I do not remember: it may be already in your hands. If you can employ an attentive person to find the Achilles, I will make him a present of a sovereign for his half-day's work. And now about the *My little Kid*. It was sent by Mr. Mackenzie to me, and by me to you, and I saw it in a proof-sheet, but not in the large number which I last returned."

[Landor was now eighty-three years old.]

17. " And now I do trust the trouble is over. The *Achilles and Helen* was not written when the *Fruit off an Old Tree* was publisht in 1853. This renders the search more easy. I hope my sovereign will bring it."

18. " Monday Morning. Your memory is good in regard to Tait. I had forgotten the name. Several other of my things are probably in his Magazine and elsewhere. My friends in town never had my Helen, they say. You tell me you are putting in type *Lauder of Milton*. It now occurs to me that a wretched imposter named *Lauder* did or wrote somewhat about Milton. Therefor the words must be

Praiser of Milton ! worthy of his praise."

[Tait's *Edinburgh Magazine* ran from 1832 to 1864. The other references in the poem are to Linton, and the line was published in accordance with the alteration here made. William Lauder, who died in 1771, published a fraudulent treatise on Milton to prove some cock-and-bull theory. He was, instead, himself proved to be a forger.]

19. " Despite all my care, and yours too, which was much greater, some verses have got into *The Dry Sticks* which are printed in the *Last Fruits*. This cannot be helped now. There they must remain. Had I kept the *Last Fruits* I might have avoided this, and so, perhaps, I might if you had sent me a *second* proof-sheet, which I could have referred to. One of my best poems, the meeting of *Achilles and Helen on Ida*, is not there, and I quite forget (as I do everything), in what periodical or paper of any kind, it was published. I will write immediately to Mr. Forster's secretary, and request him to look for it everywhere. It may come, with the two or three last Epigrams, as an

Appendix. . . . I find at this second view of the *Last Leaves*, p. 401,

'A bird was seen,' etc.

which is among those sent last by you—but it matters little if there is only one repetition."

[*A Bird was Seen* is No. 167 of *The Last Fruit off an Old Tree*, p. 401. It was removed from D.S.F. after the second proof. Some half-dozen poems in D.S.F. had appeared in whole or part, and sometimes in varied forms, in *The Last Fruit off an Old Tree*, and these are noted by Messrs. Wise and Wheeler in their Landor Bibliography. It may be observed that in the same work, in which immense care has been taken to trace the first appearance of every poem of Landor's, there is no note of any earlier publication of the *Achilles and Helen* poem than that in D.S.F.

John Forster was Landor's biographer.]

20. "Thursday Morning. Last night I ought to have stated, positively, that the Helen, etc., was sent to Taits in the beginning of the present year. The Editor, known to you, gave both you and me some trouble. After a while he sent the money, which went to its destination instantly."

21. "It is curious that neither of us should have remembered the name of Tait, when I more than once troubled you about him, and some money which he owed me for the very Helen we have been in quest of, and another thing or two. The profits of these I had promised a poor author—I never keep any for myself,

and should be very much ashamed if, when so many better men are in want, I kept 5 shillings in my pocket at the end of a quarter."

22. " I willingly give up for erasure the verses on *Crinolines*. It grieves me to have lost the best poem I ever wrote—my Helen and Achilles."

[The verses on crinolines cannot be traced. It is not in D.S.F., nor is it one of the poems cancelled in proof.]

23. " You have not printed the latin iambics on the Death of Pomero. It would add to my grief if the best of my latin verses were lost as well as the best of my English."

[The reference is to *Canis Urna*, No. 384, D.S.F., p. 229.]

24. " Tuesday Morning. I could not be happy, until I had made one more attempt to recover at least a few lines of *Helen*. Here it is—not *very* much inferior to the one lost."

25. [Nothing to be noted.]

26. " Saturday Morning. My illness stupifies me. In p. 147 I corrected in my copy, *not* in yours, the v.

> Canning, in english and in latin strong,
> Was quite an infant, etc."

[The reference is to *Our Statesmen*, No. 251, D.S.F., p. 147. The lines originally read,

> In English and in Latin one was strong,
> But quite an infant, etc.]

27. " My eyesight is so defective that I can not decipher many of the words marked in your letter.

My Homes is the title to the poem, which, as you suggest, may immediately precede *Helena*."

[*My Homes* is No. 313, D.S.F., p. 179. In the first proof it was called *Homes*.]

28. " Saturday Morning."

[Nothing to be noted.]

29. "After all. I find an error in p. 232—generos*a* should be generos*e*. I am very blind."

[The correction is in the Latin line signed S.B. on p. 239, D.S.F., among the *friendly notices* forwarded to the publisher in honour of Landor.]

30. [Nothing to be noted.]

31. " I send a few lines, written to-day, on a poet whose little volume is printed by Hogg of your city. Nothing in Scott or Burns or Keats breathes purer poetry."

[The lines are *On the Grasshopper*. *By Dunsterville Brucks*, No. 245, D.S.F., p. 142. Wise and Wheeler give the reference to a poem in *Autumn Leaves*, by George Alexander Dunsterville Brucks, Edinburgh, 1857.]

32. " . . . . you once thought somewhat might improve the Title. Here is one. Let the Printer avoid the old character, and print as follows:

DRY STICKS,
FAGGOTED BY THE LATE W. S. LANDOR."

[Whether " The late " was Landor's humour or dejection, who shall say ? He lived another six years.

The designation was not, of course, upon the title-page of the book.]

33, 34. [Nothing to be noted.]

35. "I sit up in my bed to transcribe *the* correct copy of Ad Senectam. It may be printed at the close—without any such barbarous nonsense as *Errata*, etc., etc."

[*Ad Senectam* is No. 330, D.S.F., p. 204.]

36. "Oct. 14. My eyesight must have become very defective, for I am quite unable to read a great many words in the letter I received from you last evening, with the proof-sheet. . . . Do some of the words in your letter relate to the *Title ?* I think they must—for I find many kind expressions which appear to refer to it. The Title, as now enlarged, will puzzle some; and may attract a few readers. I am highly pleased at thinking that the volume will be larger, by what I have recovered from various quarters, than it would have been with all which had already been printed, without them. *The Death of Blake* is worth all the rest. I am promised a translation into Greek of the Europa, by the only man able to perform it. . . . It was principally to avoid similarity of rhyme and subject that I wished to see an Index."

[*Death of Blake*, No. 243, D.S.F., p. 137, and *Europa* is *The Ancient Idyl*, No. 1, D.S.F., p. 2.]

37. "I am now hopeless of finding or receiving any more of my poetry. The *Achilles and Helen* is worth all of it. October 23, '75."

38. " I received last night your letter and the Criticism in the Nonjuror. It is impossible to express how gratified I feel by it. I may expect all sorts of insolence from the Edinburgh Review and from Blackwood, of whose name the last syllable seems to be spelt wrong, excepting the last letter."

JOHN COLLOP

JOHN COLLOP

TO discover a new poet is a matter for just fervour. If he be a young and living poet, the sponsor should not take too much to himself, since his man is likely enough to discover himself in time with no one's assistance. But, when he is a poet buried in the oblivion of centuries, the lucky finder may say with pride, " I did it." To bring a poet back to life is an act having in it the nicest salt of piety. But for this chance, it may be ventured, the loss of so many years might have been a loss forever.

In the *Dictionary of National Biography* is a brief entry under the names, Collop, John. No dates are given, save that he " flourished" 1660. A bare record of his three known works follows, with the information that he added M.D. to his title-pages, that he wrote often " against the puritan sectaries," and that his songs " show some lyrical capacity." That, with perhaps the unexpressed approval of a stray reader here and there, is the extent of John Collop's fame after two hundred and fifty odd years. And so it might have gone on, but that one day in Mr. Chatto's shop in Panton Street I saw a little volume on the shelf, labelled *Collop's Poems*, and took it down as my custom is, in the ever-disappointed hope that here might be a forgotten master. The title-page was—*Poesis*

Rediviva*/or/*Poesie*/*Reviv'd*/By/John Collop M.D./
Odi prophanum vulgus & arceo/London/Printed for
Humphrey Moseley, and are to be/sold at his shop at
the Princes Armes in S. Pauls/Church-yard/1656."
I opened the book at random, and was electrified by the
beginning of a poem, thus:

> Each day a market is, where we do buy
> Or unto sale expose eternity.

Owing to its extreme scarcity the book was highly
priced. It was Saturday morning, and the shop was
about to close. I did not care to risk so many pence
on scarcity alone, and had no time to investigate poetic
merit beyond that startling promise. But I was told
that I might take the book away to examine it, which
I did, and before Monday morning I was aching with
anxiety lest some hateful collector who had half
ordered the book by post should have sent his cheque,
and so have destroyed Collop and me together. At
opening hour I was there; nothing had happened.
I paid the price, and went away determined to cry
my possession abroad, and give a poet a little of his
sadly belated due.

The first friend to whom I communicated my news
was Mr. E. V. Lucas. He observed that nothing
could be done for a poet with the name of Collop (this
was indiscreet to me, who myself have poetic aspirations). But he could not gainsay the evidence, which I

---

* Collop's other poetical work, *Itur Satyricum ; in Loyall Stanzas*
(1660), is but an uninspired welcome to Charles II. at the Restoration.

now propose to put before my readers with as little digression as possible. One may write a critical essay about the poetry of Milton or Keats, but it would be pointless to write about Collop's poetry, of which the reader knows nothing. My purpose is, therefore, to give as far as possible an epitome of the book itself with liberal quotation. Perhaps later this discursive anthology may be amplified by a reprint of *Poesis Rediviva* in whole or in part.

Collop was a doctor of medicine, and freely carried his professional knowledge with him to his art. Many of his poems are loaded with anatomical conceits unintelligible to the lay mind. Also he was, as the *Dictionary* observes, an ardent scolder of Puritan or some other kind of sectaries, and although these local and occasional interests were important enough to him, they are unprofitable to us. Religious quarrels cut no ice to-morrow morning. The prevalence of party and doctrinal verses, with a cloud of dispensary fumes, makes it, indeed, very doubtful whether a full reprint of Collop's book would do him any service. He is notably a poet for careful selection, and the poems of which I am chiefly to speak are those that might be recommended to such a volume; but he was so good a writer that even his poorest pieces are apt to contain remarkable lines or passages. As will be seen, it is at the end of the book that he comes to his full stature, achieving there some half-dozen lyrics that seem to me to stand with the very best of seventeenth-century poetry.

The book contains one hundred and twenty-eight poems. Of these I have marked sixty-seven as being, on the whole, negligible. In the non-secular poems among these, religious emotion generally succumbs to theological dialectics, and, in others, political energy is diluted in a wash of rhetoric. The poet in both cases is lost in a tractarian whose day is gone. There are a few epigrams on names and books, but they mostly have intelligence without point. Throughout this group of failures, Collop, who tended always over-much to a fantastic fashion of his time, strains his conceits to stupidity, and is too often the man of medicine curiously jocular without being witty. But even at his worst he is one in a fine lyric tradition, always readable, and giving us—these from the failures —such lines as:

> Like th' mad man living in a Seaport Town,
> Thought all the ships came in the hav'n his own,

or (of Sir Thomas Browne):

> Brown other's errors, others write their own.

The first poem in the book is called *The Poet*, and is a good example of Collop at his average level, easily above his failures, but far short of his best. In a rather high-flown *Epistle Dedicatory*, in which he " presents these besprinklings of a retirement " to the Marquis of Dorchester, he says finely: " Nor is Poesie unworthy of your Patronage, which a Sir Philip Sidney hath prais'd, our Seraphick Donne us'd . . . "; and disciple-ship to Donne is marked freely on his style. His

pointed and antithetical way sometimes fails in lucidity,
but he often gives real poetic life to close-knit com-
pression; he not only brings brain work to his poetry,
he can make mere intellectual deftness poetical. This
first poem, *The Poet*, is in this manner, and at once he is
careful to justify himself explicitly:

> None are born Poets, naturally some pace,
> Shuffle in rithme, horse-like, without a grace.
> His Helicon must flow from sweat of 's brain;
> And musing thoughts lend his Poetick vein;
> Richer than those veins spring from heart of earth,
> While Gold without an Ore he giveth birth,
> Th' Philosopher's Elixir in each line,
> Doth in epitome all that's rich confine.

Not that his poetic creed is without the more airy
rapture, since—

> Poets are Prophets, and the Priests of Heav'n:
>   *   *   *   *   *
> Nor would it blasphemy be for to deny
> The whole Creation ought but Poesie.

The poem is interesting, and tells us from the first
that there is a specifically Collopian manner, but it is
not among his rarest, nor in his lesser antithetical vein
does it equal such later things in the book as this from
The Character of Loyall Friendship :

> The frost of th' times to this Corn's nutriment turns,
> Who like a torch that's beaten brighter burns:
> Can smile at all the pageantry of vice;
> Poor vertue happier think with her own price.
> To Velvet Cushions no devotion pay;
> Knows straw within, though their outsides be gay.

From this poem may be taken once for all an example of his too much precision:

> Who wants not that, which wanting, nature grieves
> Can't want, each one as much hath, as believes.

The second poem in the book, *On the Soul*, is a close philosophical argument, rising at the close from distinction to a promise of the great lyrics that are to follow. His theme here is the body a prison, with contemplation the liberator:

> Who knows himself, knows all; he's wise indeed,
> Who can retire within, and himself read.
>   *   *   *   *   *
> Let contemplation give but wings to th' soul,
> It in a moment travels to each pole;
> Descends to th' center, mounts to th' top of th' world,
> In thousand places can at once be hurl'd:
> Can fathom the universe, without touching it . . .;

and then the flame beats up, thus:

> Lord, see this bird of Paradise in a Cage,
> Assayléd by a mutinous tumul's rage.
> See th' daughter of thy bounty, heav'ns own Child;
> By passion's rabble shall she be defil'd?
>   *   *   *   *   *
> Th' King's daughter, Lord, was glorious within,
> Let not her beauty be eclips'd by sin.
>   *   *   *   *   *
> A wedding garment, Lord, on her bestow:
> Let her embroidered with thy graces go.*

---

* Collop's printer was of his kind, and it has been necessary sometimes to correct his liberties by my own. The spelling and pointing are very haphazard, and here and there a word seems to be wrongly given.

The Fruit of Paradise is the next poem, in the same manner, with a good couplet:

> While God his Saints with sanctity doth cloath,
> The figleaves of Hypocrisy they loath,

but not calling for special notice. Then come a number of the more negligible pieces, followed by *The Character*, etc., already mentioned, and a poem *To the Son of the late King*, which opens well with:

> Rule o're thyself, the World's Epitome,

but passes through indifference with an occasional witty note to a last line in keeping with the first:

> Would'st be a slave to slaves ?   Then be a King.

Two pieces of political invective follow, well written, with a knowledge of the tricks of satire, effective for their purpose, but not distinguished, save perhaps for the line:

> And looks as grave as th' man i' th' alehouse Jug.

And then we come to a poem, admirable throughout, and with one touch at least of Collop at his finest. It is *A Character of a Compleat Gentleman* and is inscribed jointly to " John Cotton Esq; Heir to the Knowledge and Virtue as well as to the Honour and Fortunes of his Ancestors," and "His Coz. George Boswel Esq; rich in Desert as in Fortune." It opens in good businesslike fashion—

> Thou to the lame art legs, eyes to the blinde.
> They their own wants in thy perfection finde.
> Thou pluck'st no houses down, to rear thy own,
> The poor God's houses rear'st out of thy stone,

and moves then by way of such wisdom as:

> For Honour, Conscience dost not put to sale,
> Or thy Religion steer by profits gale
> Imbib'st no dregs ev'n in these lees of time,
> A licenc'd ill can'st think no lesser crime,

through a growing flush of eulogy to the splendour
of—

> Thy Reason is a Hawk, which takes a flight,
> As if she'd nest her in a sphere of light.

To have watched a hawk soaring into a clear sky until
it is lost in light is to realize the magnificence of this
fusion of exact imagery with passion.

Two more examples of pointed political writing
follow, and then a charming poem *On Poverty*, with:

> While others sport of winds, hoist into th' deep,
> Along the shore he doth securely keep.
> The Ostridge's body hindereth her wings,
> While such a lark mounts up with ease and sings.
> Who desires little, he thinks little much;
> Such as desires are, ev'n our Riches such. . . .

The Pleasures of the World is good, especially in the
opening, but it is only once quite on fire (the bird that
sits and sings is a favourite figure with the seventeenth-
century poets) in—

> Pleasure's a wandering bird, doth singing sit,
> But flies away when you would catch at it.

The long *Defence of Curiosity* is rather laboured in
poetry if not in intellect, not among the poet's successes,
but with:

> More than the gamester sees the stander by;
> This life's an art of casting of the die:
> The world's the Inne, in which the cheaters meet,
> Scarce life a passage hath without deceit. . . .

and other lines to match them. Then are more pages of no consequence, with a happy phrase, as " They live long who live well," here and there, and a likelier poem *To a Painted Lady* with the lovely close:

> 'Tis neither marble, gold, nor paint,
> But the Adorer makes the Saint.

Not quite among his best, but far above the deserts of neglect, is *To His Lady Book :*

> Come, Book, my Mistress, neither proud nor coy,
> The gay nor impudent mymicks thee enjoy.
>
> * * * * *
>
> The Heav'n's a Book, the Stars the Letters be,
> Where I will spell out ridling Destiny.
>
> * * * * *
>
> A shallow puddle doth resemblance bear
> Of Sun, Moon, Stars, and all Heav'n's glory there:
> Yet with a finger you may fathom it. . . .

And with it may be placed *On Retirement,* which follows, with a very fine passage:

> Thus I can pinion time, memory recruit;
> From th' age snatch th' sickle, and reap Wisdom's fruit.
> In th' scheme of th' world my own Nativity finde,
> And there gain eyes to see where Chance is blinde.
> The fool is solitary, wise man ne're alone,
> Who hath himself, wants no companion.
> Who serves himself is never serv'd amisse:
> Retirement Wisdom's Cousin German is. . . .

Then for a dozen pages there is little to note save a few couplets, as for example—

> Our minde the day is, and our flesh the night,
> Death is but darkness, and our life the light . . .

which might have been but isn't quite first-rate, and comes in a too ingenious poem *Man a Microcosm*. Preceding another relatively poor group is a short poem, *The Poetaster*, very good, with an opening that is perhaps the best part of it:

> All are not Poets, who can pace in Rime,
> And to an odde tune can in ding dong chime;
> Castalian nymphs and God Apollo name;
> Don Cupid's fire, and a Sea-froth'd dame:
> While they glean straw in Egypt for to raise
> Unto themselves strange pyramids of praise.
> Though like to tulips they enamel'd be,
> Yet the fool's Coat is their best Liverie. . . .

Then there is a strange little group of fantastical love poems, in praise of *A Yellow Skinned Lady*. They have a lyric grace, and in spite of their strange occasion there shines through their absurdity a thin ray of passion—

> Sure 't is some Phoenix here must build a nest,
> She hath both flame and spices in her brest,—

the passion that was to flower so beautifully under fitter use.

Collop adds to these others of a like kind on variant themes—*An Ethiopian Beauty, On a Crooked Lady, The Praise of Thick and Short, To Dionysia the Plump*

Lady, and so forth. Again they are elegantly turned, but the Rabelaisian note not infrequently falls into mere unpleasantness, and the verses have little more than a freakish interest. The best of the lot are *On Monocula, A One Ey'd Lady*, in which a rather ugly conceit is very gracefully employed, and to a lady *Contemning her Age*, with *The Answer*, where his bearing just saves the poet from a certain brutality. By way of these we come to a few love lyrics of the more usual inspiration, and these are for the most part done with an ease that matches the best of the Cavalier love songs, mingled now and again with a deeper note that looks forward to the religious lyrics in which he claims kinship with the poets who walked in ways unknown to Carew and Suckling and Rochester. *The Praise of his Mistress* is good enough to quote in full, as are also *On a Retir'd Lady* and *To a Lady Singing, Mistake Me Not*. This is from the first-named:

> Admire no more those downy breasts
> Where Candor's pure Elixir rests.
> Praise not the blushings of the Rose,
> Which th' morning's mantle doth disclose:
> Nor subtile Lillies which out-vie
> Calcining art's choice Chymistry.
>   *   *   *   *   *
> For if my Mistress but appears,
> The sullied snow turns black with tears:
> Swans seem to wear the veil of night,
> And blushing Lillies lose their white,
> The bashful Roses drooping die,
> Bequeathing her their fragrancy.
>   *   *   *   *   *

> Thus meaner beauties patches are,
> Spots, nay foils to make her fair.
> These lesser lights dimm'd by her eye,
> Twinkle, go out in stench, and die.
> If you would know who this may be,
> I neither know, nor eye e're see.

This is not notably above the average level of the better love lyrists of the time, but it is excellently not below it, and it is by a man who has been allowed no share of their fame; it is, moreover, a good deal below his own best. One other quotation from this group—the first and last couplets from *On a Refin'd Lady*—

> Choice extract of thy Sex, where we
> May finde what's in it good in thee:
> *   *   *   *   *
> Who'd folios of thy Sex read o're,
> Since in Epitome he findes more ?

It is the kind of thing that, when all has been said for and against it, remains with the advantage of being well written. *To Eugenia, a Defence of Juvenile Wildness*, is a good example of Collop's intellectual deftness. The plea of " wild youth " to his mistress is made with a subtlety and niceness that would have delighted the " seraphic Donne ":

> Myrabolans and dates in bloom, and bud,
> Both noxious are, both in their fruit are good.
> *   *   *   *   *
> Know barren earth doth mines of gold obscure:
> And viler shells do precious gems immure.
> Come, my Eugenia, thou shalt me refine;
> See how from dirt doth spring a glorious mine !

and in another poem to Eugenia, there is:

> I will not say that swans hatch in your breast,
> For innocence there doth keep a whiter nest,

which is an admirable case of Collop's imaginative use of words, if we remember the idiom of the age. Passing by one or two deft renderings from Horace, and a rather overwrought poem of some length against a widow's " devotion to relicks," and leaving the love poems, a word must be said of *A Palinode. On a Resolution to do Penance with Ashes*, in which the promise of a passage at the opening is hardly fulfilled:

> Since dust to dust we all must go
> He's wise who timely can do so.
> Thus I bequeath myself to th' grave
> While death and I ev'n portions have.
>
> Thus holier Hermits choose their cells,
> An Anchoret in his grave thus dwells.
> The Nun views death's head, book, and grave,—
> Thus they have all, who nothing have. . . .

This may also be said of the poem *On Marriage*, an interesting essay in philosophical argument, in which the conceits and rather conventional thought are to be set against a good beginning (Collop is full of good first and last lines), and such flashes as—

> As Saints to Altars, so to bed repair,
> Love hath his Altars, bring chast off'rings there.

On the World is a telling piece of savagery, full of drive, with—

> Who is no monster doth a monster seem:
> 'Tis only prosperous vice men virtue deem . . .

for its text.   *On Our Father* is an excursus on the
Lord's Prayer, close and significant, in which ingenuity
becomes poetry in its own manner.   It is followed by
Incerta poenitentia, with its " Each day a market is,"
already quoted, and *Certamors*, in which the note of
sureness that has been sounding through the book
seems to be on the point of full achievement, a promise
which is redeemed on the next page, in the poem
On the Resurrection.

After a short Latin poem there are then eight poems
left, and in at least six of these Collop touches a height
of which it would be difficult to speak in terms of extravagance.   It cannot but be that to know of the
beauty that is here will henceforth be to allow its
maker his fitting immortality.

On the Resurrection is in six seven-line stanzas.
These are the first and last:

> Arise, my God, my Sun arise !
>   Arise, thy side
>   My sin doth hide;
>   Thy blood makes pure,
>   Thy wounds me cure,
> He ever lives, who with thee dies:
> Arise, my God, my Sun arise.

> *   *   *   *   *

> Come thou Abyss of sweetness, come:
>   Come my dear Lord.
>   Say but the word
>   Unto my Soul,
>   I shall be whole.
> Thou for thyself mak'st onely room:
> Come thou Abyss of sweetness, come.

Here is the larger note of the age. It is followed by
The Leper Cleans'd, a great religious lyric, opening
superbly, and moving with assured mastery to a close
which is as wonderful as anything in seventeenth-
century poetry. This poem must be given in full—
it is interesting to note the variation in design midway
through the poem, so unexpected and so successful:

> Hear, Lord, hear
> The Rhet'rick of a tear:*
> Hear, hear my brest;
> While I knock there, Lord take no rest.
>
> Open ! ah, open wide,
> Thou art the door, Lord, open; hide
> My sin; a spear once entered at thy side.
>
> See ! ah, see
> A Na'man's leprosie !
> Yet here appears
> A cleansing Jordan in my tears.
>
> Lord, let the faithless see
> Miracles ceas'd, revive in me.
> The Leper cleans'd, Blinde heal'd, Dead rais'd by thee.
>
> Whither ? ah, whither shall I fly;
> To heaven ? My sin, ah, sins there cry !
> Yet mercy, Lord, O mercy ! hear
> Th' atoning incense of my prayer.
> A broken heart thoul't not despise.
> See ! see a Contrite's sacrifice !

---

* If Collop remembered Shirley's—

> " If thy face move not, let thy eyes express
> Some Rhetorick of thy tears to make him stay . . ."

(*Narcissus*, 1646), he at least bettered good instruction.

Keep, keep, viols of wrath, keep still:
I'll viols, Lord, of Odors fill:
O prayers, sighs, groans, and tears a shower,—
This precious ointment forth I'll pour.
I'll 'noint, wash, wipe, kisse, wash, wipe, weep;
My tears, Lord, in thy bottle keep.
Lest flames of lust and fond desire,
Kindle fresh fuel for thine ire,
Which tears must quench, like Magdalene
I'll wash thee, Lord, till I be clean.

This is followed by *The Good Samaritan*, a poem of almost equal beauty; and then *Vox poenitentiae*, good but not with the greater lyrics; and then again a thing of exquisite completeness, *Spirit, Flesh* :

S.   Arise, make haste.
F.   Whither ? ah, whither flies my soul so fast ?
S.   Heav'n calls; obey.
F.   'Tis night; ah, stay ! 'tis night ! thou'l lose thy way.
S.   The day springs rose.
F.   Ah, but thy sin black clouds doth interpose.
S.   Those penance clears.
      The sun succeeds a sacred dew of tears,
        See, a full shower !
      Heav'n suffers violence by a holy Power.
F.   Ah, Heav'n is high !
S.   Prayer lends a Jacob's ladder to the sky,
        Angels descend.
F.   Wrestle, ah wrestle ! Blessing crowns the end.

Soul and Christ and *Of Prayer*, which come next, are good enough to honour any poet's reputation, but a shade perhaps below these others of Collop's best. They are followed by *To the Soul*, which is as magnificent as *The Leper Cleans'd* and an addition forever to English poetry:

> Dull soul, aspire.
> Thou art not earth, mount higher;
> Heav'n gave the spark, to it return the fire.

> Let sin ne'er quench
> Thy high flam'd spirit hence—
> The earth the heat, to Heav'n the flame dispense.

> Rejoice, rejoice,
> Turn, turn each part a voice;
> While to the heart-strings tun'd ye all rejoice.

> The house is swept,
> Which sin so long foul kept:
> The peny's found for which the loser wept.

> And purg'd with tears,
> God's Image re-appears.
> The peny truly shews whose stamp it bears.

> The sheep long lost,
> Sin's wilderness oft crost,
> Is found, regain'd, return'd; spare, spare no cost.

> 'Tis Heav'ns own suit,
> Hark, how it woo's you to 't:
> When Angels needs must speak, shall man be mute?

The book ends with a short poem *On the Nativity*, striking the right note, though not in its greater exercise, a worthy conclusion to the whole.

As I have suggested, if Collop's work were easily accessible and known to readers, more might be said of his technique: the very stubborn quality of his verse, for instance, and his careless fondness for double couplets on the same rhyme, of which I have counted a dozen examples in his book, with one triple pair, and of his frequent and friendly use of proverbial speech—as "necessity hath no law," "what though a rouling stone gathers no mosse," "marriage and hanging both are destiny," "else nothing's so but as our fancies are." But my object has been to give as far as possible the measure of a hitherto unknown—or forgotten—poet, by some wealth of example. Collop was an occasional poet in a sense, in the sense that many of his best contemporaries were. That is to say, he did not devote either his time or his meditation chiefly to poetry, as Milton did. But he was not an occasional poet in the lesser sense; he did not have to wait upon occasion for the matter of his verse. As a poet he was preoccupied with two or three groups of subjects—political, amatory, religious; and his imagination could return to them at will. To his poetry he could bring energy and comprehension always, and at intervals he could rise to a lyric greatness that might have instructed Herbert (and Herbert often gets far less than his due from critical opinion), that Crashaw would have saluted, and to note which Vaughan himself might have paused by the way. Such a one cannot remain with oblivion.

A POEM BY CHRISTOPHER SMART

A POEM BY CHRISTOPHER SMART

THE Rev. Thomas Seaton, who died in 1741 at the age of fifty-seven, placed the following clause in his will, dated October 8, 1738:

"I give my Kislingbury estate to the university of Cambridge for ever: the rents of which shall be disposed of yearly by the vice-chancellor for the time being, as he the vice-chancellor, the master of Clare-Hall, and the Greek professor for the time being, or any two of them, shall agree. Which three persons aforesaid shall give out a subject, which subject shall, for the first year be one or other of the perfections or attributes of the Supreme Being, and so the succeeding years, till the subject is exhausted; and afterwards the subject shall be either Death, Judgment, Heaven, Hell, Purity of Heart, etc., or whatever else may be judged by the vice-chancellor, master of Clare-Hall, and Greek professor to be most conducive to the honour of the Supreme Being and recommendation of virtue. And they shall yearly dispose of the rent of the above estate to that master of arts, whose poem on the subject given shall be best approved by them. Which poem I ordain to be always in English, and to be printed, the expense of which shall be deducted out of the product of the estate, and the residue given as a reward for the composer of the poem, or ode, or copy of verses."

At one period Christopher Smart may almost be said to have acquired a proprietary right to the Seatonian Prize, having won it in 1750, 1751, 1752, 1753, and 1755, and no doubt missing it in 1754 only because he did not compete for it, getting married at that time instead.

The following poem has, at least, the interest of being addressed to Seaton's memory. The best that can be said of any of Smart's work other than the *Song to David* is that it reminds us at moments of that great poem. Perhaps the sympathetic reader will detect a phrase or two of which as much may be said in these lines, which are not to be found in any collection of Smart's work.

ON GRATITUDE

To the Memory of Mr. Seaton

O Muse ! O Muse ! Voice & Lyre,
　Which are together Psalm of Praise
From heav'n the kneeling bard inspire
　New thoughts, new grace of utt'rance raise;
That more acceptable with Thee
　We thy best service may begin
O thou that bent thine hallow'd knee,
　Had bless'd to bleed for Adam's sin.
Then did the Spirit of a Man
　Above all height sublimely tour,
Had the sweet Gratitude began,
　To claim Supremacy from Pow'r.
But how shall we these steps ascend,
　By which the Host approach the Throne ?
Love thou thy brother and thy friend,
　Whom thou on earth hast seen & known.

For Gratitude may make the* plea
  Of Love by sisterhood most dear—
How can we reach the first degree
  If we neglect a step so near ?
So shall we take dear SEATON's part
  When paths of topmost heav'n are trod,
And pay the talent of our heart,
  Thrown up ten thousand fold to God.
He knew the art the World dispise
  Might to his Merit be applied
Who when for man he left the skies
  By all was hated, scorn'd, denied.
†" The man that gives me thanks & laud
  Does honour to my glorious name "
Thus God did David's works applaud,
  Had seal'd for everlasting fame.
And this for SEATON, shall redound
  To praise, as long as CAMUS runs;
Sure Gratitude by him was crown'd,
  Who bless'd her Maker & her Sons.
When SPENCER virtuous SYDNEY prais'd
  When PRIOR DORSET r hail'd to heav'n;
They more by Gratitude were rais'd
  Than all the NINE & all the SEV'N.
Then, O ye emulative bribe
  Of Granta, strains divine persue;
The glory to the Lord ascribe,
  Yet honour SEATON's memory too.
The *Throne* of EXCELLENCE accost
  And be the post of Pray'r maintain'd;
For Paradise had ne'er been lost
  Had heav'nly Gratitude remain'd.

CHRISTOPHER SMART.

---

* 1 John iv. 20.   † Ps. i. 23.

ERASMUS DARWIN

ERASMUS DARWIN

"THE BOTANIC GARDEN"

ERASMUS DARWIN, the grandfather of the great Charles, was born in 1731 and died in 1802. He spent most of his life as a doctor at Lichfield where once he seems to have met Johnson, twenty years his senior. As, however, the elder Darwin was, as Sir Leslie Stephen says, a free-thinker and a radical and a dictator in his own circle the meeting was not a success. He seems to have been a sober and upright man, " confining himself," again in Stephen's words, " to English wines, possibly to minimize the temptation to excess," but he is the hero of a story told by Miss Seward which describes him as in a state of " vinous exaltation " swimming the river with his clothes on and thereupon mounting a tub in the local market-place to address the people on prudence and sanitary regulations. He earned the tribute of a poem from Cowper, a stanza of which runs:

> We, therefore, pleas'd extol thy song,
>   Though various, yet complete,
> Rich in embellishment, as strong
>   And learned as 'tis sweet.

Darwin's song was certainly learned; never, perhaps, has the English muse been so loaded with learning in

her life.   It is called *The Botanic Garden*, and it had its
origin in a copy of verses addressed by Miss Seward to
Darwin, "complimenting him on his sequestered
retreat near Lichfield.   In this retreat there was a
mossy fountain of the purest water; aquatic plants
bordered its summit, and branched from the fissures
of the rock.   There was also a brook which he widened
into small lakes.   The whole scene formed a little
paradise, and was embellished with various classes of
plants, uniting the Linnean science, with all the charm
of landscape."   Darwin told Miss Seward that she
ought to make her poem "the exordium of a great
work.   The Linnean system is unexplored poetic
ground, and a happy subject for the muse.   It affords
fine scope for poetic landscape; it suggests meta-
morphoses of the Ovidian kind, though reversed.
Ovid made men and women into flowers, plants, and
trees.   You should make flowers, plants, and trees into
men and women.   I will write the notes, which must
be scientific, and you shall write the verse."   But the
Swan of Lichfield was not to be caught with chaff,
and so Darwin was left to carry out his great design
in its entirety himself.   In 1791 he published *The
Botanic Garden.   A Poem, in two parts.   Part I.
Containing the Economy of Vegetation.   Part II. The
Loves of the Plants.   With Philosophical Notes.*   No
author's name appeared on the title-page.   The
second part of this volume, *The Loves of the Plants*,
had really appeared first, having been published
in 1789, and as part of the 1791 volume it appears

in its third edition. The work as a whole takes an extremely distinguished place among the best bad books in the language.

The poem is something over four thousand lines in length, and the notes are considerably more than twice as long as the poem. The publisher was J. Johnson of St. Paul's Churchyard, and he presented Dr. Darwin in a very handsome quarto volume, finely printed, and containing several beautifully drawn botanical plates, as well as more general illustrations including a very fine one of the fertilization of the Nile, engraved by Blake after Fuseli.

The scheme of the poem is monumental. The first part is a scientific account of the creation of the vegetable world, profusely embellished with classic allegory. The second part is an elaborate personification of something like a hundred flowers in succession, designed in accordance with the Linnean classification, thus: "The classes are distinguished from each other by this ingenious system, by the number, situation, adhesion, or reciprocal proportion of the males in each flower. The Orders in many of these Classes are distinguished by the number, or other circumstances of the females." With these characteristics in mind our poet treats of the amatory adventures of each flower in the way suggested to Miss Seward, and in almost every case he adds a supplementary fable. Here is an example, Vitis being the Vine, the flower of which, the note tells us, contains five stamens or males and one pistil or female.

" Drink deep, sweet youths," seductive Vitis cries,
The maudlin tear-drop glittering in her eyes;
Green leaves and purple clusters crown her head,
And the tall Thyrsus stays her tottering tread.
—*Five* hapless swains with soft assuasive smiles
The harlot meshes in her deathful toils;
" Drink deep," she carols, as she waves in air
The mantling goblet, " and forget your care."—
O'er the dread feast malignant Chemia scowls,
And mingles poison in the nectar'd bowls;
Fell Gout peeps grinning through the flimsy scene,
And bloated Dropsy pants behind unseen;
Wrapp'd in his robe white Lepra hides his stains,
And silent Frenzy writhing bites his chains.

So when Prometheus braved the Thunderer's ire,
Stole from his blazing throne etherial fire,
And, lantern'd in his breast, from realms of day
Bore the bright treasure to his Man of clay ;—
High on cold Caucasus by Vulcan bound
The lean impatient Vulture fluttering round,
His writhing limbs in vain he twists and strains
To break or loose the adamantine chains.
The gluttonous bird, exulting in his pangs,
Tears his swoln liver with remorseless fangs.

This passage is characteristic of Darwin's general design, and the verse is about at his average level. The poem as a whole is said once to have been very popular, though it is inconceivable that many people at any time can really have read it. Darwin, as we shall see, was sometimes not a bad poetical theorist, but as a poet he is the supreme master of misdirected energy. His first advertisement tells us that " the general design of the following sheets is to enlist Imagination under the banner of Science; and to lead her votaries from the looser analogies, which dress out the imagery of poetry, to the stricter ones which form the ratiocination of philosophy." Whatever may be said for or against the principle, never was design more fatally carried out. Minutely specific knowledge combines with an orgy of stilted and inflated abstraction to make the poem pretty nearly everything that poetry should not be. And, of course, the seeds of deadly ridicule were in the subject itself. Whatever pretensions the work as a whole may ever have had of poetic achievement were destroyed by Canning in his *Loves of the Triangles*, in this manner:

> In filmy, gauzy gossamery lines
> With lucid language, and most dark designs,
> In sweet tetrandryan, monogynian strains,
> Pant for a pistil in botanic pains;
> Raise lust in pinks and with unhallowed fire,
> Bid the soft virgin violet expire.

This is really hardly better than Darwin himself at times, for example

> Hence glows, refulgent Tin ! thy chrystal grains,
> And tawny Copper shoots her azure veins. . . .

Or

> Go, gentle Gnomes ! resume your vernal toil,
> Seek my chill tribes, which sleep beneath the soil.
> With ceaseless efforts rend the obdurate clay,
> And give my vegetable babes to day !

Or

> So the lone Truffle, lodg'd beneath the earth,
> Shoots from paternal roots the tuberous birth;

which last is from Darwin's other work, *The Temple of Nature*, published in 1803, consisting of another heavily annotated two thousand lines, this time upon organic life.

Darwin's work, however, in spite of its passionate ineptitude, is far from being without interest, and this not merely a negative interest. I have recently read it all through, sometimes with a good deal more than perverted entertainment, even with admiration. Leslie Stephen notes that when the worst has been said by way of disparagement, it is " remarkable that Darwin's poetry everywhere shows a powerful mind." This is justly observed, and it is a mind that for all its shortcomings is nearly always engaging company. Darwin was, as Cowper said, really learned, and although he was a poor hand at translating his learning into song it does leave us impressed even while we laugh. And in the notes which, as has been pointed out, exceed the poem itself in length, this learning finds its natural expression and is often instructive in a quite delightful way. Darwin's book was published, it must be remembered, in 1791. " As the specific levity of air," he says in one of his notes, " is too great for the support of great burthens by balloons, there seems no probable method of flying conveniently, but by the power of steam, or some other explosive material; which another half century may probably discover," and he is rather apt at such scientific guesses at truth. His poetry and his notes alike are a compendium of correct and

incorrect information. We believe him when he tells
us that:

Unknown to sex the pregnant oyster swells . . .

but not when he tells us that the oil of clove instantly
relieves slight toothaches. He makes out a very
effective case for the hygienic properties of hot baths
as against cold for people of advancing years, which is
consoling; but it may be a little discouraging to adventure to be told that "As many families become
gradually extinct by hereditary diseases, as by scrofula,
consumption, epilepsy, mania, it is often hazardous
to marry an heiress, as she is not unfrequently the last
of a diseased family." It is genuinely interesting to
learn from his notes on the Alphabet that "polite
people" of his time pronounced glove—dlove, and
Cloe—Tloe; but after being told that "it has been
proposed to produce a luminous music, consisting of
successions or combinations of colours, analogous to a
tune. . . . This might be performed by a strong
light, made by means of Mr. Argand's lamps, passing
through coloured glasses, and falling on a defined part
of a wall, with moveable blinds before them, which
might communicate with the keys of a harpsichord;
and thus produce at the same time visible and audible
music in unison with each other," we are scarcely
surprised to hear that "the execution of this idea
is said by Mr. Guyot to have been attempted by
Father Caffel without much success." The experiment has, I believe, been renewed in our own time,

but Mr. Heath Robinson would seem to be its most likely sponsor.

As a critic of the art of poetry our doctor must after all appear with but one passage only. Speaking of the difference between prose and poetry, in one of his entertaining dialogues between a bookseller and a poet, which form interludes between the cantos of *The Loves of the Plants*, he says: " Next to the measure of the language, the principal distinction appears to me to consist in this: that poetry admits of but few words expressive of very abstracted ideas, whereas Prose abounds with them. And as our ideas derived from visible objects are more distinct than those derived from the objects of our other senses, the words expressive of these ideas belonging to vision make up the principal part of poetic language." He then gives a quite shrewdly chosen illustration, thus, " Mr. Pope has written a bad verse in the *Windsor Forest :*

And Kennet swift for silver Eels renown'd.

The word renown'd does not present the idea of a visible object to the mind, and is thence prosaic. But change this line thus,

And Kennet swift, where silver Graylings play,

and it becomes poetry, because the scenery is then brought before the eye."

Darwin's reconstruction may not do quite what he claims for it, but there is sense in what he says. Unfortunately, as we have seen, the principle he lays

down is precisely the one that he most dismally failed
to observe in his own verse, but in parting it must be
said that our pleasure in his book does sometimes
come from the verse itself. The learned and eloquent
mediocrity is just now and again relieved by a note
that lends authority for a moment to Cowper's
flattery that Darwin's song was sweet as well as learned.
It may be an odd line here and there, as

> The misty moon withdrew her hornèd light,
> And sunk with Hesper in the skirt of Night . . .

or

> With airy lens the scatter'd rays assault,
> And bend the twilight round the dusky vault . . .

where for a moment Darwin does seem to fulfil his
intention of enlisting imagination under the banner
of science. Or it may be in longer passages such as the
rather fine description of the rape of Europa in *The
Economy of Vegetation*, which, however, I will omit in
favour of three short passages which seem to me to
show Darwin at his best. The first is from the second
canto of *The Temple of Nature* and tells of the angels
coming to Abraham.

> So when angelic Forms to Syria sent
> Sat in the cedar shade by Abraham's tent;
> A spacious bowl the admiring Patriarch fills
> With dulcet water from the scanty rills;
> Sweet fruits and kernels gathers from his hoard,
> With milk and butter piles the plenteous board;
> While on the heated hearth his Consort bakes
> Fine flour well kneaded in unleaven'd cakes.

> The Guests ethereal quaff the lucid flood,
> Smile on their hosts, and taste terrestrial food;
> And while from seraph-lips sweet converse springs,
> Lave their fair feet, and close their silver wings.

The following is, again, from *The Economy of Vegetation* :

> She comes !—the Goddess !—through the whispering air,
> Bright as the moon, descends her blushing car;
> Each circling wheel a wreath of flowers intwines,
> And gem'd with flowers the silken harness shines;
> The golden bits with flowery studs are deck't,
> And knots of flowers the crimson reins connect.—
> And now on earth the silver axle rings,
> And the shell sinks upon its slender springs;
> Light from her airy seat the Goddess bounds,
> And steps celestial press the pansied grounds.

This is very pretty, and Darwin seems to have thought well of it himself as he did something of the same sort of thing some years later in *The Temple of Nature*, and with no less success.

> Delighted Flora, gazing from afar,
> Greets with mute homage the triumphal car;
> On silvery slippers steps with bosom bare,
> Bends her white knee, and bows her auburn hair;
> Calls to her purple heaths, and blushing bowers,
> Bursts her green gems, and opens all her flowers;
> O'er the bright Pair a shower of roses sheds,
> And crowns with wreathes of hyacinth their heads.—
> —Slow roll the silver wheels with snowdrops deck't,
> And primrose bands the cedar spokes connect:
> Round the fine pole the twisting woodbine clings,
> And knots of jasmine clasp the bending springs;

Bright daisy links the velvet harness chain,
And rings of violets join each silken rein;
Festoon'd behind, the snow-white lilies bend,
And tulip-tassels on each side depend.

At the end of his last dialogue with the bookseller, Darwin says of his *Botanic Garden:* " Such as it is, Mr. Bookseller, I now leave it to you to desire the Ladies and Gentlemen to walk in; but please to apprize them, that, like the spectators at an unskilful exhibition in some village-barn, I hope they will make Good-humour one of their party. . . ." I trust I have not done our botanic poet less honour than this.

HARTLEY COLERIDGE

HARTLEY COLERIDGE

I.

HARTLEY COLERIDGE, the eldest son of Samuel Taylor Coleridge, was born on September 19, 1796, and was thus four years younger than Shelley and a year younger than Keats. In the collected edition of his poems, published in 1851, there is a portrait of him at the age of ten done by Sir David Wilkie. It is the picture of a sad, not unhumorous little face: with large affectionate eyes, very beautiful but not promising much resistance to the onsets of a hard world. In the collected essays, published in the same year, there is another portrait of Hartley taken not long before he died in 1849. The hair is white and the eyes have fulfilled their promise, and the humour and melancholy have taken on an air of gentle scholarship, but the face is strangely that of a child still, a child masquerading, it might be, as a kindly and very intelligent little old man at a mumming. And this child-like character was the thing that most impressed all Hartley's acquaintances from first to last. Everybody admitted his wide though loosely organized learning, and there is cumulative evidence that his conversational gifts were quite unusual, but however genuinely he was admired he was still the admired child. His failings were treated by his friends with what seemed to be a perfectly natural indulgence. His father regarded him always with the tenderest affection, but always as an infant, or as Derwent Coleridge, Hartley's younger brother, puts it in his admirable *Memoir*, "in some sort an infant still." The excited sensibilities of childhood never left him; "He could not open a letter without trembling." After his Oxford misfortunes (he lost a Fellowship through intemperance, as we shall see) "he was still a pure-minded, single-hearted, child-like being, in whom everyone felt an interest,—over whom *almost* every one was ready to have a care, viewing his aberrations with a peculiar compassion, as if from some mysterious cause he were not fully responsible for his actions." Writing to his mother when he was thirty-five, he says that he has an instinctive horror of big boys, perhaps derived from the persecution that he suffered from them when he was a little one. His father in a codicil to his Will, with touching solicitude made special provisions that he should not come to want through innocent improvidence, but it should be added that Hartley's life, though it may have been irregular in some ways, was frugal enough in its habits. "He was remarkably fond of the travelling shows that occasionally visited the village," says one friend of Hartley when he was over forty years of age. "I have seen him clap his hands with delight; indeed, in most of the simple delights of country life, he was like a child." And another writes: "There was about him a child-like and confiding spirit, a oneness and simplicity, which bore witness to Wordsworth's wondrous penetration when he predicted that Hartley would retain

> by individual right,
> A young lamb's heart among the full-grown flocks.

And, finally, another correspondent writes to Derwent: " When he was in merry mood, he was as gay as a three years child. . . . It is no uncommon thing to see an old man with hair as white as snow, but I never saw but one—and that was poor Hartley—whose hair was mid-winter while his heart was as green as May."

Hartley's actual childhood was spent among the English lakes, partly at Keswick, at Greta Hall, with his Uncle Robert Southey, partly in a school at Ambleside. Samuel Taylor was a little uncertain about his domestic responsibilities, but there was always a beautiful devotion between him and his eldest son. When the older poet died in 1834, Hartley wrote to Derwent: " What with my irregular passions and my intellect—powerful, perhaps, in parts, but ever like ' a crazy old church clock and its bewildered chimes '—what but for him I might have been, I tremble to think. But I never forgot him; no, Derwent, I forgot myself too often, but I never forgot my father." Before going to the Ambleside school, Hartley when he was eleven spent a summer with his father, partly in London going to some theatres and visiting the Tower with Walter Scott, and being instructed in chemistry by Humphry Davy, partly at Coleorton as the guest of Sir George Beaumont, Wordsworth also being of the party, and partly

at Bristol with Grandmother Fricker, whose daughters
Sara and Edith had married Coleridge and Southey
respectively. Southey's kindness to the Coleridge
children was in keeping with the character of a man
whose gifts and virtues have been somewhat stifled by
his epics.

The boy Hartley, like other children, had his own
little world of make-believe, but with a difference.
He did not content himself with brief and casual
inventions, but contrived a world—he called it
Jugforcia, or alternatively Ejuxria—peopled it, gave
it a constitution, a geography, armies and international
relations, and lived in it continually, writing or relating
its history from day to day. The extreme facility of
improvisation that here displayed itself never left him,
and was no doubt all his life in conflict with the harder
and more exact qualities that are needed for creation
of the highest kind. It was a gift that charmed his
friends, but all his life he proved how dangerous a gift
it can be to a poet.

In 1815 he obtained a scholarship or post-mastership
to Merton College, Oxford, and in due course got a
second in Greats, his placing, it is said, being due to a
compromise between the examiners, some of whom
wanted to give him a first and others, as Derwent says,
a fourth. But the good opinion of him prevailed when
a little later he stood for an Oriel fellowship and was
elected handsomely. He had, however, first to pass the
usual probationary year, and the result was calamitous.
He was liked, he was eager to please, he was greatly

talented, he was affectionate and gracious, but he was incurably shy with the young men whom he had to teach, he became nervously introspective, he drank more than was good for him, and at the end of his probation he was deprived of his fellowship. " Great efforts were made to reverse the decision. He wrote letters to many of the Fellows. His father went to Oxford to see and to expostulate with the Provost. It was in vain." The blow was one that reverberated through the rest of Hartley's life. It did not break him, and although he never quite outlived the dangers from which it came, he was never mastered by them, and his character remained as pure as that of the other poet who had been sent down from another College in the High Street some ten years before his own dismissal. There is little more to be said of the events of Hartley's life. He spent his days in the country of his childhood, moving from Grasmere to Nab Cottage at Rydal for his later years, the intimate friend of Wordsworth, beloved by the Westmorland dalesman or " statesman," earning a sufficient pittance for his needs (with modest help from his mother) by poetry and occasional criticism for the reviews and publishers, and ending his gentle life when he was just over fifty years of age, not at all worn out but the victim of bronchitis. He is buried in Grasmere churchyard, close to the Wordsworth grave.

Hartley inherited from his father a habit of marginal annotation, and in his copy of Anderson's *British Poets* in thirteen volumes he left a copious running commentary upon what was his favourite reading. Of Richard West, the poet who was with Gray at Eton, he says: " Some writers maintain a sort of dubious, twilight, existence, from their connection with others of greater name. R. West, though an elegant and promising youth, is one of them. He would have been forgotten had he not been the friend of Gray. Jago would have no place among poets had he not been a favourite of Shenstone. Kirke White will live by the kindness of Southey. If aught of mine be preserved from oblivion, it will be owing to my bearing the name of Coleridge, and having enjoyed, I fear with less profit than I ought, the acquaintance of Southey and of Wordsworth." Although the suggestion that has occasionally been made that, taking them both at their best, Hartley is ever near the poetic rank of his father, is clearly misguided, the estimate that the younger poet here makes of his own powers is well on the side of modesty. His verse, which first appeared in a thin volume printed at Leeds in 1833 and now rather scarce, collected in 1851 by Derwent Coleridge in the two volumes above mentioned, and added by Mr. Ramsay Colles to the Muses' Library in the present century, has very considerable merit. It reflects the poet's tender and whimsical personality very faithfully, and it shows a fine natural gift of versification carefully developed. Hartley could write, and he knew how not to be dull. His poetry is not a leading example of anything in particular, but it has the great merit of being very readable and bearing the test of good

company. In his prose Hartley's natural diffuseness
of character is more apparent. His lighter essays on
set themes, although they are not without happy
turns, remind us to their disadvantage of Charles
Lamb. Wit could not be laboured with so exquisite
a deliberation twice in an age. But in his essays on
poets and poetry Hartley rarely travels more than a few
sentences without saying something that can bear
comparison with the best things of critics more uniformly excellent than he. If his gait were more certain
he would be among the most accomplished of critical
essayists; as it is we have to watch him with some
indulgence between his finer moments, but the indulgence does not tax us too severely and there are handsome compensations. In prose Hartley on the whole
does himself most justice when he is allowed to address
a subject in his own leisurely way, as in the essays *On
the Character of Hamlet* and *On Parties in Poetry*.
In these will be found an agreeable fancy, good sense,
and good English. There are more favoured writers
who have less to recommend them.

II.

I.

[Thomas Hood, to whom this letter is written, was
editor of *The Gem* from 1829, and in the issue for that
year printed two of Hartley's poems, the lovely *She
is not Fair to outward View*, and the sonnet *It must be so*,

my Infant Love must find. These, no doubt, are the contributions offered in this letter.

The editor of *The London Magazine* at this time was Henry Southern. Hood may have effected the necessary introduction; if so he did it promptly, as the November number of that magazine in 1828 contains Hartley's *Isabel* (there called *Lines on the Death of a Young Lady*) and the *Reply*, with the following editorial comment:

Would that such men as Hartley Coleridge, and his brother Derwent, and one or two others of the same little knot of strong and natural thinkers, would write more, and drive such pretenders from the field, as we sometimes see puffed into a reputation which is perfectly ridiculous].

" SIR,

"I hope the trifles I herewith enclose will not be too late, to obtain a place in your miscellany— if you think them worthy of insertion. Should you produce a second number, I may, if my present efforts meet your approbation be a larger contributor. Could you favour me, by informing me, who is the present editor of *The London Magazine* and whether an article or two would be acceptable, or if there be any other periodical in want of journeymen ?

"I remain Sir

"Yours truly

"HARTLEY COLERIDGE.

"GRASMERE,

"*October* 4, 1828."

2.

[This letter is not dated by Hartley, but as his father died on Friday, July 25, 1834, the following Tuesday, on which the letter was written, would be July 29. It is addressed to — Graves, Esq., Thorney Hows (?).]

" DEAR SIR,
    " Since I last saw you I have received intelligence that my revered father is no more.   He departed this life at ½ past six on Friday morning last.   He had suffered much, but died calmly, testifying the depth and sincerity of his faith in Christ.
    " Of course I am in no state of mind for society— and you will excuse me from waiting on you according to your kind invitation.   Little thought I while [?] on so wildly, that my parent was even then a corpse— I trust—a blessed spirit.
                              " Yours truly
                                 " H. COLERIDGE.
" TOWN END.
    " Tuesday."

ROBERT STEPHEN HAWKER

ROBERT STEPHEN HAWKER

I.

"AND shall Trelawny die?"—of the many readers to whom the line is familiar, there are probably but few who know anything of its author or the rest of his work. Not, indeed, that its author was exactly its author; he happened, as poets will, upon an admirable burden, stole it, and immortalized it in a perfect setting.

Robert Stephen Hawker was very much, as our old writers would have said, a "Character." Born some generations deep of ecclesiastical stock, he himself took orders on leaving Oxford, and in 1834, at the age of thirty, became Vicar of Morwenstow, in North Cornwall, a charge that he retained until his death more than forty years later. At Oxford he won the Newdigate prize with a poem on Pompeii, but left without other academic distinction, taking, it seems, a pass degree. His, life thereafter was spent far away from centres of polite, or indeed any, learning, and on that sublime but terrible coast, of which an inhabitant said that only twice in sixteen years had the sea been calm enough to reflect a passing sail, he moved in something of prophetic isolation, a devoted parish priest, very jealously the father of his flock, a figure unusual enough, but too unconcerned for attitudes, and a poet of uncertain but sometimes rare genius.

He thought ordinary clerical clothes dull, and he found them unsuitable for ministrations among the stormy rocks of his parish. So he wore a claret-coloured cassock coat over a blue sailor's jersey, fishing boots above the knee, and a plum-coloured or pink beaver hat. When he wore gloves, as he commonly did both in and out of church, they were of crimson. For an overcoat he used a large yellow blanket, a hole cut in the centre to go over his head. On his jersey was a little red woven cross, symbol of one of the sacred wounds, and always tied by a string to a button-hole of his coat he carried a pencil. Thus equipped he walked or rode about his missions, usually accompanied by a black Berkshire pig, " well cared for, washed, and curry-combed." Inquisitive comment on his apparel was met with a solemn assurance that it perpetuated the habit of the primitive Cornish Church, or that his coat was that of " an Armenian archimandrite."

The Morwenstow country is likely to retain its untameable character in spite of all change, but in Hawker's prime, the days of rudimentary roads and transit, it was not only wild but almost inaccessible. Here the stubborn but sensitive spirit found his call a lonely one, and the society in which he ministered was no less difficult than the natural features of his rounds. Hawker was a High Churchman, and his general disposition of goodwill did not allay the suspicion and mistrust of a population largely Wesleyan and Bryanite. He was openly impatient of dissent however generous he might be to dissenters, and his humour probably did not go very well when on it being supposed by the minister of another denomination that he would not be willing to bury one of his dissenting parishioners, he replied that on the contrary he should be delighted to bury them all. And his lay relations with the Morwenstow inhabitants were even more troubled. He was loved by the labourers and the poor, as well he might be, but the landowners and employers showed active resentment against this queer fellow who was always menacing their privileges. These were days when farm-labourers thereabouts were paid sixteen shillings a fortnight, fourteen shillings of which was paid not in cash, but in measures of corn, and of the balance a shilling a week was taken for rent. Hawker asked how his people were to buy clothing, and fuel, and boots, and food other than corn, on nothing a week, and for half a lifetime he stormed and begged his way through continual crises of poverty among his flock, while privilege crossed him in every way it could, as may be supposed. " Fifteen years I have been vicar of this altar; and all that while no lay person, landlord, tenant (employing tenant he means), parishioner or steward, has ever proffered me even one kind word, much less aid or coin. Nay, I found them all bristling with dislike. All the great men have been hostile to me in word or deed."

But his reward in gratitude from the poor themselves never failed. " They are crushed down, my poor people, ground down with poverty, with a wretched wage, the hateful truck system (payment in corn), till they are degraded in mind and body." And to relieve this suffering he spared nothing. Hard winter nights would see little, sometimes, indeed, very formidable, expeditions of charity setting out from the vicarage, often to the serious impoverishment of Hawker's own household. He would suddenly bethink him of some cottage with no resources against the pitiless Cornish weather, and off he would carry or send a blanket or a pie or a bottle of wine or brandy. As one of his emissaries recollected it, " It isn't once, it's scores o' times, he's looked out o' window . . . at night and shouted to me: ' Here, stay, come back, Vinson,' and he's gone into the larder, and cut off great pieces of meat, and sent me with them, and p'raps brandy or wine, to some poor soul; and he always gi'ed me a shilling, either then or next day, for myself, besides meat and drink."

It was stern stuff that carried on this work in such conditions for forty years. Nor did Hawker's ministry lack the more romantic rigours. His Cornish coast is grimly famous for its wrecks; hardly a generation before his time it had also been notorious for its wreckers. It was no longer the thing to thrust drowning sailors back into the sea and concentrate wholly on the incoming salvage, but the wild scenes on the seashore in which our poet so often took a part stirred, we may be sure, ancestral emotions in some of the participants. The ghoulish terrors had departed, but

Hawker still would at times be met with sullen indifference as he rode in haste along the coast beseeching the fishermen to take out their boats.   And even when the rescue work went forward with a will, the drama was fantastically tragic enough.   Here is Hawker's own account of one disaster, to an East Indiaman: " Crew thirty-two, six saved alive, twenty-six drowned.   The channel is full of wreck-cargo—and among it corpses. Thirteen came ashore at Bude at the time of the wreck, some lashed to the raft. . . .   We have lived in continual horror ever since—*i.e.*, in sad and solemn expectation of the dead.   Accordingly on Tuesday, the 4th, the message came at night. 'A corpse ashore, sir, at Stanbury Mouth.' . . .   My lych house cleared and a plank or two laid to receive the dead. A message.   They are nearly come.   I go out into the moonlight bareheaded, and when I come near I greet the nameless dead with the sentence—'I am the Resurrection and the Life.'   They lay down their burthen at my feet.   I look upon the dead.   Tall, stout, well-grown, boots on and socks."   Then a coffin, and two days' delay before the law provides the warrant to bury, " and by that time the poor dissolving carcass of Adam, seventeen days dead, has so filled the surrounding air, that it is only by a strong effort of my own, and by drenching my men with gin (for bearers) that I can fulfil that duty which must be done. . . ." And then another body, and another, and " when all is done, it is not without a battle that we can win from the county rate about 30s. a corpse—for each interment the balance, always £2 or £3, coming from my own purse. And I have this day buried my thirtieth sailor in the seamen's burial-ground by the upper trees."*

Hawker lived to be over seventy. He married twice, first, when he was still at Oxford, a lady twenty years his senior, and secondly, when he was over sixty, a Polish lady by whom he had three daughters. His was a busy, if lonely life. Like most really happy men, he was for all his humour subject to periods of profound melancholy, and his sturdy convictions were not above waywardness. A silly parson asked him what were his " views and opinions." Hawker pointed out ·from his window to the Atlantic, the crags, and the church with its yard—" These are my views; as to my opinions I keep them to myself." In politics he voted as he felt at the time, now distressed at a Conservative defeat, now recording that " it will always be to me a source of pride, that I was the first, or well-nigh, I think, the only clergyman in this deanery who voted for a Free-trade candidate." He had an inspired reverence and affection for the fabric of his ancient Morwenstow church, but he was less than fastidious about litter and dirt inside it. His curate one day could bear it no longer, and swept up the debris himself surreptitiously, " old decorations of the previous Christmas,

---

* This account is taken from J. G. Godwin's preface to the first collected edition of Hawker's poems published in 1879. For other biographical details I am indebted to Mr. S. Baring-Gould's *Vicar of Morwenstow*, a book severely criticized for inaccuracies that by no means make it worthless.

decayed southernwood and roses of the foregoing midsummer festivity, pages of old Bibles, prayer-books and manuscript scraps of poetry, match-ends, candle-ends, etc." He thereupon conveyed his vicar's shame in a wheelbarrow to the parsonage door. Hawker met him, and on being told that this was the rubbish from his church, requested the curate to complete the pile by sitting on top of it, when he would have it properly attended to.

The sturdy life was harassed at the close by poverty and ill-health. For a time Hawker took opium, and for a time he conceived that he must subsist entirely on a diet of clotted cream, which made him sick. Mr. Thomas Hardy, who had long wished to make the acquaintance of the Cornish poet, remembers going to Morwenstow in 1875, intending to call on him, and on arrival hearing the passing bell announcing Hawker's death, which had taken place at Plymouth. Immediately before his end, when he was in a state more or less comatose, Hawker was received into the Roman Church—a somewhat mysterious circumstance that gave rise to much unseemly wrangling at the time. What the truth of the matter was we do not know, nor did its interest survive the pious bigots whom it so much concerned. It was an event that had nothing to do with Hawker's robust and picturesque heyday or with his poetry. The Hawker we care for was he who said to his friend Godwin that he should like his poems to be preserved for his children that they might know their father by them, that they might remember, in his own lovely phrase, that " he had good images once in his mind."

The close student of nineteenth-century verse has had ample opportunity of becoming familiar with the bulk of Hawker's poetry. It was issued in a series of small volumes, the first of which (after the prize poem) was *Tendrils* by Reuben, 1821, to be followed by *Records of the Western Shore*, 1832, *Ecclesia*, 1840, *Reeds Shaken with the Wind* (first and second series), 1843-44, *Echoes from Old Cornwall*, 1846, *The Quest of the Sangraal*, 1864. These little books have all become scarce, but less so than the single sheets on which Hawker was in the habit of circulating his verses. In 1869 these various publications were brought together in one volume as *Cornish Ballads and Other Poems*, reprinted in 1884. There have also been collected editions of the poems, edited respectively by J. G. Godwin, in 1879, by Alfred Wallis, in 1899, and by C. E. Byles, in 1904. To call Hawker an unlettered poet would be absurd, but he was a poet who wrote away from the world of letters. At his best he was none the worse for that, but when the pressure of his gift was low he was not very exacting with himself, and there was no neighbourly authority, as it were, to keep him up to standard. So that at times he wrote verses much as another parson might compile his parish magazine. Even so, Hawker's magazine would be a superior one, but we hardly want to turn over its pages again. A good deal of his verse is, in short, commonplace. But a little of it is anything but commonplace, and gives Hawker a secure enough holding among the little nineteenth-century classics. The Trelawny ballad is as good as it can be, and poems like *Datur Hora Quieti* and *The Southern Cross* have just the distinction of style that is lacking in much of his work; while *The Dirge* and *A Christ-Cross Rhyme* seem to me to be pure enchantment. His one long poem (other than *Pompeii*), *The Quest of the Sangraal*, has a fine roll and colour, but little of Hawker's peculiar reality or his finer vision. It is an accomplished and very readable exercise. But in his fortunate moments—and Hawker was a poet of moments—such as have witness in these few pages, Hawker joins his own company of Cornish Fathers, celebrated in lines that he prefixed to *Echoes from Old Cornwall* and afterwards incorporated in *The Quest of the Sangraal*—

> They had their lodges in the wilderness,
> Or built them cells beside the shadowy sea,
> And there they dwelt with Angels, like a dream:
> So they unroll'd the volume of the Book,
> And filled the fields of the Evangelist
> With thoughts as sweet as flowers.

I am indebted to Mr. Frederick J. T. Headon for the following communication. The poem does not appear in Hawker's works.

"11, COLLINGHAM ROAD, S.W. 5.
"24 *April*, 1924.

"MY DEAR SIR,
"Mr. E. C. Byles, the son-in-law of Robert Stephen Hawker, the Cornish mystic and poet, has told me that you contemplate a work on Hawker,

and I am writing you about a short poem that has come into my possession, which Mr. Byles or myself don't think has ever been published so far. I copy it here:

> My love is like a wintry flower
>   That blossoms on a Tomb
> Let thy sweet Bosom be the Bower
>   To fold its latest Bloom !
>
> No other hand shall touch a leaf,
>   'Twill bear no other eye,
> The strongest Love is born of grief
>   Its fondest breath, a sigh !

"You will notice that these lines, though graceful enough, are hardly up to his highest standard, but they are interesting biographically, and would have come in well for the *Life* (had they then been known), in the chapter on his second marriage—that is, if they were written about 1864.

"These lines are written on a half sheet of paper, the special red-lined paper he was so fond of, and in his bold writing, but the MS. is not dated. It was given to me on my pilgrimage to Morwenstow last September, by an old lady that Hawker knew as a child, almost the only person left now who remembers the Vicar of Morwenstow.

"If you think it worthy of your work, I see no reason why you should not use it as an unpublished poem. Perhaps you would let me know ?

"Yours faithfully,

"FREDK. J. T. HEADON."

WILLIAM BARNES

WILLIAM BARNES

I.

WILLIAM BARNES, a Dorset man by long descent, was born in the country known as the Vale of Blackmore in 1801. He lived to be eighty-six years of age, and his long life was spent partly as a schoolmaster in Dorchester and elsewhere, and partly as Rector of Winterborne Came, a parish on the fringe of the county town. Walking to-day in the main street of Mr. Hardy's Casterbridge, the visitor will see beyond the church palings that stand along the pavement a beautiful little memorial to Barnes, showing the venerable poet in the figure that has not yet wholly passed from living memory. There he stands, bareheaded, with his long beard, a cassock falling over his knee-breeches, allowing us to see the stockings (black silk we are told they were) and low strap shoes. His characteristic dress, as to the shape and tones of which he was fastidious, reminds us for a moment of the other parson-poet of a nearly neighbouring county, but his benign gravity had nothing of the touch of rugged eccentricity that was part of Hawker. It is true that by a pleasant whim of taste Barnes also affected an overdress made of a simple cloth with a headhole, and he liked red hats—though certainly not Popish ones. But Barnes, who was a

saint, was also charmingly a little of a dandy, and he
anticipated Mr. Worth in taking hints from nature for
the hues of his raiment, sober as it was, while the silk
stockings showed to advantage legs that his daughter
in her affectionate memoir confirms the poet's portrait
in describing as comely.

As a country schoolmaster and priest Barnes from all
records was clearly of an ideal tenderness, simplicity,
and devotion that would have satisfied Oliver Gold-
smith.   But he was also a very learned man, and almost
a Crichton in accomplishments.   " Nothing came amiss
to him," says his daughter, " from making garden
arbours and carved chairs for his wife, and dolls'
cradles and carriages for his children, to the turning
out of Latin epigrams." He invented a swimming
apparatus, a quadrant, an instrument for describing
ellipses, he played the flute, the violin, the piano, and
the organ, he turned his own chessmen, he had a good
baritone voice, he went fishing, and he helped General
Shrapnel in calculations concerning that worthy's shell
—of these and other achievements we learn from the
same authority.   But, less casually, he was a philologist
of great originality and reputation, with a knowledge of
many languages, and all through his life he was engaged
in philological research that resulted in a long and
important series of publications.   The Dorset dialect—
or language, as he claimed—was his chief study, and
the most enduring witness to his erudition in this
sphere is to be found in the three volumes of *Poems
of Rural Life* (published respectively in 1844, 1859, and

1863, and collected into one volume in 1879), by virtue
of which he holds a highly distinguished place among
the little group of dialect poets that this country has
produced.

Of these dialect poems Mr. Thomas Hardy has
made a selection published by the Oxford University
Press, and in his introductory essay he discusses Barnes's
dialect art with unrivalled authority. But while
Barnes in his poetry usually employed the Dorset
dialect, which came to be a poetical instinct with him,
he also wrote a good deal of verse in national English,
to use his own term, and this has been undeservedly
neglected. The selection published by Mr. Blackwell
in 1925 serves as a reminder of its merit. In 1864,
soon after the publication of the third series of dialect
poems, the editor of *Macmillan's Magazine*, in paying
Barnes for a contribution, suggested to him, no doubt
with a good deal of reason, that he was seriously
limiting his audience by writing in a speech that was
not easily intelligible to the general reader. The
result was that the poet prepared for publication a
fourth series of poems of rural life, this time in
" Common English." The book was published in
1868, with a little note in which Barnes says:

" As I think that some people, beyond the bounds of
Wessex, would allow me the pleasure of believing that
they have deemed the matter of my homely poems
in our Dorset mother-speech to be worthy of their
reading, I have written a few of a like kind, in common
English; not, however, without a misgiving that what

I have done for a wider range of readers, may win the good opinion of fewer."

But Barnes had, in fact, as far back as 1846, two years later, that is, than the appearance of the first dialect series, published a volume of poems in this same national English, so that the 1868 book was not wholly due to a fresh impulse from outside. In 1870 appeared yet another volume of non-dialect poems, a little privately printed pamphlet of twenty-four pages.*

The first of these volumes (1846) contains little that shows Barnes at his best. Most of the work in it is rather tamely descriptive, or simple in its emotion almost to the point of commonplace. Some of the best passages are in a series of alliterative experiments, but the obtrusiveness of the experiment, for me at any rate, becomes tiresome and obscures the merit. The book also contains a number of sonnets, a form that Barnes used with little effect, and one that he had no care for in his later work. Rarely in the 1846 volume is there a poem that leaves a memory once the page is turned; *Whitburn's Green and White* is, I think, the most successful piece in the book. But the collection of 1868 is another matter altogether. Some of the

* The full titles of Barnes's six volumes, not including the collected dialect poems, are as follows:— (1) *Poems of Rural Life, in the Rural Dialect: with a Dissertation and Glossary.* 1844. (2) *Poems partly of Rural Life, in National English.* 1846. (3) *Hwomely Rhymes. A Second Collection of Poems in the Dorset Dialect.* 1859. (4) *Poems of Rural Life in the Dorset Dialect. Third Collection.* 1862. (A double title-page, one showing the date 1863.) (5) *Poems of Rural Life in Common English.* 1868. (6) *A Selection from Unpublished Poems.* 1870.

poems here seem first to have been written in dialect, and "translated"; Mr. Hardy in his selection prints five poems as hitherto unpublished which are versions of poems that appear here in "Common English," and he also chooses four of the "Common English" poems themselves from this book, but does not otherwise represent Barnes in this manner.

Barnes was no untutored minstrel; he was, indeed, a highly skilled technician, weaving all sorts of structural fancies into his verse. "Primarily spontaneous, he was academic closely after," says Mr. Hardy, and the characterization is as true—and in the same sequence —of his "Common English" as of his dialect verse. Barnes had a lyric heart, but he was a grave gentleman, a scholar, and in the most agreeable sense a precisian, and he delighted to exercise his singing gift in the terms of a very agile and conscious art. It will be noted, too, that this poet who as a parish priest had more than an amateur knowledge of the seamy side of life, chose to be unashamedly on the side of the angels in his poetry. His uncompromising "goodness" may shock some of the sturdier critics of a younger school who would no doubt style as shallow and sentimental his pronouncement that "there is no art without love. Every artist who has produced anything worthy has had a love of his subject. . . . A scorn of the subject produces satire; therefore satire, however clever, is no more true art than a caricature is an artistic paint-ing." How surely some of our psychological lions would riddle that, and how shrewdly they would measure the timorous spirit of whom it could be written that " he would eschew all the evil in newspapers." But the old poet who on his deathbed at eighty-six, feeling rather better one morning, wrote a poem, and a very good one, out of lightness of heart, would laugh tolerantly at them. He liked to tell the story of a man to whom he made a joke about a donkey, and who on meeting him some time after said, " I do never see a donkey, sir, but what I think o' you." Goodness with men who have this humour comes not of easy ignorance, but of deep and often tragic knowledge, and it is goodness of such character that is the theme of Barnes's very carefully deliberated poetry.

II.

[The following three letters, written to the Rev. G. Herbert West, of Ascham School, Bournemouth, give a pleasing glimpse of Barnes's archæological enthusiasm. He was eighty-three when they were written.]

I.
" THE RECTORY,
" WINTERBORNE CAME,
" DORCHESTER.
" 7 *June,* 1884.

" REV. SIR

" I give my best thanks to you and Mrs. West for your kindly given invitation to Luncheon on the 18th of June but I believe I cannot have the pleasure of joining the Field-club on that day.

" I am
" Rev. Sir
" Yours very truly
" WM. BARNES."

2.

" CAME RECTORY,
" DORCHESTER.
" 16 *June,* 1884.

" REV. SIR

" From your generous invitation to the Dorset Field-club to luncheon with you I believe you take an interest in their work and hope you will kindly forgive me if I ask you a simple question or two about Christchurch. Asser in his *Life of King Alfred* says that after his sickness at Winchester he went and stayed some time with the King at the Royal Vill called Leonaford. Now I have thought that Leonaford was at Christchurch. It is clear to me that it is British name in Welsh of our day Llionfordd, Llion being the plural of Lli a Flowing or Stream and Llion is often applied to that part of a river over which the Tides flow and ebb, a Fleet, though it seems to be given also to river streams, as I think in Llion, Lyons in France so ' y Llionfordd ' or ' y ffordd-y-Llion ' would mean the Road over the Tide streams or the Fleet. Now do you happen to know whether Alfred had a manor (Hâm) at Christchurch and whether there is a road (now I suppose bridged) over either of the rivers within the reach of the tides ? Begging you to forgive my troubling of you.

" I am
" Yours truly
" W. BARNES."

3.

" THE RECTORY,
    " WINTERBORNE CAME,
        " DORCHESTER.
            [*June* 26, 1884.]

" DEAR SIR

" I thank you very much for what you have so kindly written in answer to my questions. It is worth much instead of nothing as you thought it. I believe you have hit on the British Llionfordd in Beaulieu. If it was a ' Beau lieu ' to the Norman Kings, I suppose it was also a ' Fair place ' to Alfred and his fore elders of the old Saxon throne-stead. Winchester, of course Christchurch, and every spot of which Christchurch people have to speak to each other by a name, had a name to Britons of the place; and since it cannot be the ' Leonaford,' I believe, as I have ere now thought, that it was the ' Boluelauniam ' of the anonymous Geographer of Ravenna, since I seem to see under the Latin form of the name the British ' Bylalawan ' the Edge or Brink of the water-lily stream. For the Latin Alauna was I believe the Stour river; and ' Alan ' in Welsh is a water-lily.

" This however wants further thought.

" I should have been most happy to meet and hope that I may ere long fall in with you.

" I am

" Dear Sir

" Yours very truly
            " W. BARNES."

MR. WISE'S " ASHLEY CATALOGUE "
VOLUME IV

MR. WISE'S "ASHLEY CATALOGUE"

Volume IV.

I AM fourth in the line of Mr. Wise's ushers, and the thunder of praise in general terms has been stolen by my predecessors. The two hundred and fifty copies that have been printed of each of the first three volumes of the *Ashley Library Catalogue* have now found their way over the world, and have brought from collectors general acknowledgment of the fact that on his chosen ground Mr. Wise is Eclipse.

The mystery of book-collecting is one the members of which do not argue about their faith. I have been told by a scholar and a lover of the Muses that he would as soon read Herrick in a modern reprint at a shilling as in the *Hesperides* of 1648, printed for Mr. John Williams and Mr. Francis Eglesfield, and to be sold at the Crown and Marygold in St. Paul's Churchyard. Very well, I wouldn't. And if my friend thinks, as doubtless he does, that I and those like me are a little weak in the head in supposing that there is any essential virtue in the first issue, perfect condition, and the uncut copy (which he almost certainly thinks is the unopened copy), I should like to lead him quietly into Mr. Wise's library and leave him to the gentle and healing influence of the treasures that he affects to scorn. He

would lay no violent hands on them; they would per-
suade him. In a little while he would not only love
literature, which he already does, but also learn how
fragrant an emphasis of character literature can take
on under the auspices of the bibliographer and bibliophile. As I have said, we do not argue about our
faith, but we know it to be pledged to the not least
profitable part of scholarship.

Mr. Birrell and Sir Edmund Gosse have both con-
fessed to the sin of covetousness when confronted
by Mr. Wise's Arabia. I am not affected so. When I
am with humbler collectors, I could find it in my heart
to spoil them of their treasures. The parable is
remembered. The desires of the collector are as
strong in me as in any man, but in Mr. Wise's presence
they are paralyzed. I can imagine myself going home
from him one evening in a hypnotic trance, filling
the carpet bag that I should borrow from Sir Edmund
with my own poor pennyworth, and stealing back to
Heath Drive, the burglar of a new dispensation.

The particular glories of this the fourth instalment
of Mr. Wise's catalogue are the Popes, the Priors, and
the Rossettis. The data for the study of each of these
poets are here organized as they never have been
before. It is not only that several items, in some cases
actual discoveries, now recorded have hitherto been
practically unknown to students and collectors.
Mr. Wise's library is, it is true, bewilderingly rich in
these *introuvables*. In the case of Pope, for example,
an ordinary stout fellow among collectors might have

acquired the *Essay on Criticism* and the rare parts of the *Essay on Man;* he might even have achieved *Windsor Forest* and the *Ode on St. Cecilia's Day.* With great luck and a little money at the right time, he might have joined company with Mr. Wise among the elect for a moment with the *Verses upon the Late Duch-ss of M——* and *A Sermon against Adultery.* Then Mr. Wise marches off with *The Narrative of Dr. Robert Norris, A Blast upon Bays, A Full and True Account of a Horrid and Barbarous Revenge, A Further Account of the Most Deplorable Condition of Mr. Edmund Curll,* and *God's Revenge against Punning,* and he marches alone. But, as I say, these impossibilities, while they give a unique strain to the character of Mr. Wise's library, are not its real distinction. For the library is a superb memorial of all that is best in English literature, or, chiefly, English poetry. And so with Pope, we remember that when all is said and done the most important things about him are the *Essay on Criticism, The Rape of the Lock,* the *Essay on Man,* the *Moral Epistles,* and *The Dunciad.* And of all of these Mr. Wise has lovely copies, and of variants where they exist. Moreover, he has examined them with unrivalled bibliographical skill, and now gives us the result of many years of patient and scholarly research. For this truly is scholarship. The notes contained in this volume upon the *Essay on Criticism* and the *First Satire of the Second Book of Horace,* for example, may seem of no great consequence to the uninformed, but they are a real contribution to that orderliness of knowledge which has always been the pursuit of disinterested learning. Perhaps the most important bibliographical entry under Pope is that of the numerous editions of *The Dunciad* of 1728. Every book-collector fancies himself as something of a bibliographer, just as every man thinks he is a good judge of character, and, unless he be a Pussyfoot, a good judge of wine. But *Dunciad* bibliography is almost a career in itself, and I can only admire Mr. Wise's success, and flee, with the observation that his arguments seem to me to be quite convincing. The note about *The Progress of Dulness*, on p. 29, is a very good example of the way in which he can establish a point with disconcertingly unexpected evidence.

Mr. Wise's Priors are even richer in rarities than his Popes, and among them is an instance of another service that Mr. Wise often does to his subject, in the hitherto undescribed and unreprinted *Pindarique*. As it happens, the poem is not a very good one, but that is Prior's fault, not Mr. Wise's. With Rossetti, Mr. Wise's pre-Raphaelite triumph, to which Sir Edmund Gosse has so happily referred, is complete— no, not complete, as Swinburne shows in the later volumes of this catalogue. The ordinary collector, possessing good copies of Rossetti's 1870 and 1882 volumes, together with the *Early Italian Poets*, might think that he had done well enough. Let him turn to this catalogue and realize his inadequacy. Here are entered over a score of books and pamphlets, all of them possessing some special interest. A few even of the rarer ones may still be found, but many of them exist on Mr. Wise's shelves, and there alone, save for the copies happily preserved in the Fitzwilliam Museum at Cambridge. The Rossetti entries are further greatly enriched by the series of extremely interesting and important letters now printed for the first time. It is such things as these that make Mr. Wise's catalogue not only of the highest bibliographical value, but also enchanting to read.

Of the other riches in the present volume no more than a word can be said. Here is Ruskin, with, among other things, some newly published and significant letters to Swinburne; here are Nicholas Rowe and Elkanah Settle; here is Edward Ravenscroft, Gent, with ten plays (I wonder whether I shall ever read them); and here, finally, is a very attractive little collection of Allan Ramsay's exceedingly scarce first editions. The bibliographical value of all these entries is greatly enhanced by the facsimile reproductions with which Mr. Wise has so generously illustrated his work.

The condition of Mr. Wise's books has been generally remarked upon, as it could not fail to be by anybody with an eye and a sense of touch. Wherever possible his copies have been preserved in their original bindings, a first article of faith with all good collectors, but even Mr. Wise cannot always command the past, and a striking feature of his library is the beauty with which Mr. Arthur Calkin, of Messrs. Rivière and Sons, has exercised his binder's skill on a large number of the volumes. Bookbinding is one of the crafts that demonstrates how decidedly the trained professional, when he is encouraged by custom and works unconsciously in a long tradition, excels even the most gifted amateur. Rivière of Bath started binding books nearly a hundred years ago, and, although Bath moved to London, the work has, so to speak, been going on in unbroken succession on the same bench ever since. The result can be seen nowhere better than in Mr. Wise's library.

In conclusion, I must express a personal gratitude to Mr. Wise—which is, I know, shared by book-collectors everywhere—not only for having shown what the devotion and judgment of one man can do in a lifetime in the way of making a great library, but also for the unfailing generosity with which he administers his stewardship. His knowledge is everybody's property, and of its kind is the finest knowledge of our generation. To be stumped, as one often is, for a fact when doing a piece of work is merely to ring up "Hampstead——." Moreover, I could tell of many an engaging little packet of duplicates and such things, that have had their very satisfactory uses, but that might embarrass Mr. Wise. But I do know that when you have seen the shelves of his library, you have not seen all. I doubt whether anybody has. I have a suspicion that the real truth about the missing Shakespeare manuscripts has not yet been told.

THE LIBRARY OF A MAN OF LETTERS

THE LIBRARY OF A MAN OF LETTERS*

IT would be to make no extravagant claim for Sir Edmund Gosse to say that he is to-day the most eminent living English man of letters. It would be idle to contend about his place in any particular branch of literature. One opinion may hold that he is chiefly distinguished as a critical essayist, another that his shrewdest gift is for biography, another that he is not at the moment duly recognized for the poet he is. But all would agree that no living writer in England is so conspicuous an example of the honour that can be achieved by a lifelong devotion to literature, by loving books in all seasons and becoming their master, by drawing from them not pedantry, but a continual refreshment of life—in short, by being first and last a man of letters.

Of the patient discipline and scholarship with which Sir Edmund Gosse has served his fine natural gift as a writer, bringing it to its present easy grace and mastery, this is not the place to speak. But we have before us a volume that tells, very delightfully, of the books that have been his friends and servants on the way. Being a writer with no fantastic confusion in his mind about life and literature being separate things, but

* *The Library of Edmund Gosse*, compiled by E. H. M. Cox. With an Introductory Essay by Mr. Gosse. (Dulau and Company.)

one who has always known that literature is life, he has naturally collected about him copies of many— not most, since only the Bodleys can do that, but some thousands—of the best books in the language; we should say languages, but this catalogue deals with English books only. And being also a man with a sense of style in his tastes as well as in his writing, he has been careful in the choice of his copies, sensitive to size and condition, compromising with his purse and opportunity at times, as all collectors must, but fondling no " ragged regiment " heresies. His philosophy has been the sound one of being content with the best copy he could get, but hoping that it might be the best to be got. His active concern being with good literature, he has brought into his company many obscure books with the famous ones. And so his library has the three-fold character of being representative, of containing many rarities, and of being able to look the bibliophile in the face.

In his Introduction to the third volume of Mr. T. J. Wise's great *Ashley Library Catalogue*, Sir Edmund Gosse speaks of having " spent a lifetime plucking an overblown rose here and a fading lily there in the fields just outside the inner garden of bibliography." It is true that Mr. Wise's splendours are apt to crumple the courage of his rivals, but Sir Edmund need not be desolated, for he has many brave blooms in his own enclosure. Here, for example, are Daniel's *Delia* of 1592 (the second issue, apparently, not the first, as Mr. Cox claims), the famous Westmorland manuscript

of Donne's poems (which even Mr. Wise cannot have),
a presentation copy from Mr. Hardy of the first edition
of *The Dynasts*, with the very rare 1903 title-page to the
first volume, a great run of Jeremy Taylors, and such
modest but distinguished trivia as Leigh Hunt's *Ultra-
Crepidarius*. These are stray entries noted at random,
but the conscious pride of Sir Edmund Gosse's library
is to be found in the superb series of quarto plays
of the Restoration theatre, a pride that is none the
less conscious because, as their owner provokes us by
boasting, he secured nearly all these thin and elegant
volumes, many of which are now worth a day of Mr.
George Robey's salary, for a maximum of half a crown
apiece. But Whistler reminded the court that it had
taken him thirty years to learn how to throw his pot
of paint at the canvas.

Sir Edmund Gosse's Introduction to his catalogue
is an essay in his best manner. Any general reader
who may suppose that a catalogue of books is a special-
ist's affair and not for him is mistaken. If he should
care to be admitted into the intimacies of a very
distinguished literary life, here is his opportunity.
In the catalogue itself he will become acquainted
with the shelves that have for many years been for
Sir Edmund Gosse the familiar index of his mind,
and in the *Essay in Apology* he will find a precise
and loving survey of the moods that have gone to their
furnishing. The reminiscences that Sir Edmund
here gives us of his early British Museum days, of the
old London bookshops, of such bibliophilic cronies as

Lord de Tabley, "hanging about Red Lion Square at six in the morning, waiting for Salkeld to take down his shutters," of dramatic conflicts in the sale-rooms, make up a perfect chapter of autobiography by a writer who with *Father and Son* took his place among the assured masters of that most precarious of literary arts.

The compilation of the catalogue has been carried out by Mr. E. H. M. Cox. It is his first essay in bibliography, and, by what have been necessarily casual tests, he seems to have done credit to himself and the library under his inspection. Nothing is easier than to find errors in such work when it is done, nothing much more technically difficult than to do it. Even that prince of bibliographers, Mr. Wise, has been known to nod, so that Mr. Cox need not be discouraged if his critics detect a fault here and there in his definitions and collations. He tells us, for example, that " unless definitely stated to the contrary, all the items are first editions, but the debated question of issues has often been left in abeyance "; but he sometimes is a little vague as to the distinction between edition and issue—*e.g.*, in the *Delia* above referred to, and occasionally he falls into actual error in his order of priority, as in his description of Akenside's *Pleasures of the Imagination* of 1744. These are trifles, however, and do not detract from the painstaking ability with which he has performed a very difficult task.

It remains to be said that Sir Edmund Gosse has himself adorned several of the entries with very engaging notes.   The most striking of these is perhaps the one appended to the record of FitzGerald's *Omar*, the now almost fabulous first edition of 1859.   The entry reads: " 4to.   Half-morocco.   January, 1859. Bound with above is the Second Edition, 1868."   And Sir Edmund's note is as follows:

" This volume is the saddest in my library, for when I bought these two pamphlets they had their covers and were absolutely uncut.   I knew no better than to have them bound by an ignorant binder, who stripped off the priceless brown-paper covers and cropped the virgin pages.   I bought them in 1869."

With which poignant narration we leave him happy in his great possessions, but we go shaken by a very megrim of sympathy.

A MEMORY OF GEORGE D. SMITH

A MEMORY OF GEORGE D. SMITH

STAYING while I was in New York no more than a perilous Fifth Avenue crossing from his shop in Forty-fifth Street, I found myself constantly with G. D. S., to invest a few dollars (we collectors never spend our money, we invest it) and to refresh my contented but sometimes tired mind. I went once or twice without seeing him, so that on our first meeting I had established myself as a customer, insignificant enough in the affairs of this Napoleon of booksellers, but still a customer. And to be interested in a customer was a long half of his secret. We took to each other at once—at least I am sure I took to him, and I can but suppose, from the way he dealt with me then and thereafter, that he did to me. Every other day or so when I was in the city I spent half an hour with him, growing in admiration of the man and his sweeping vitality, floundering always in delightful temptation, delivering myself usually at a generous discount, and forming a friendship that I promised myself was to be a long and treasured one.

He reminded me always of some great comic hero out of Molière. It has been said of G. D. S. that he had no care for literature, that he was concerned only with books. It is true enough, but it did not matter. He was not the only bookseller of whom it could be said, but, unlike some of the others, he made no bones about it. And yet books were no dull commodities of sale for him; they were all glamour and romance, as surely as poetry or the prophets might be to another man. He was that way by nature, hardgrained though he may have seemed to those who knew him slightly or only as competitors. I have never known a man of more finely adventurous instincts; he had imagination, the kind that was in Scapin and Peer Gynt. He did not care for literature, it is true. He had hardly any thought of it. But he might have cared very deeply for it; he had the right temper. It pleased me to fancy that he enjoyed my friendship the more in that I was a maker of books as well as a collector. As he showed me an immaculate copy of the 1645 Milton or an uncut Gray's *Elegy* in the original wrappers, suggesting that these were by the lowest standards better than any government stock, I could, I thought, detect a touch of wistfulness, as though he knew that in these things there were yet further delights that he had not time to share. I know that when a certain work of mine pleased him I felt that it was just the sort of public that was very much worth while.

On entering his shop it was hardly necessary to inquire whether G. D. S. was in. One felt it. I suppose no bookseller could ask for a better staff than his, and yet he was a man who would have fretted with a staff of bibliophilic angels. He wanted to do everything himself, and when he was on the premises there was something in the air that told you he was doing everything. I imagine that there must have been chaos for a time after his death, so much special knowledge about his immense stock did he carry in his head. I am sure that it was a distress to him that he could not deliver his own parcels. He had the heart of a genius in bibliography—I have heard him describe with touching affection how in the early days he discovered his golden land under the direction of that aristocrat of collectors, Beverley Chew. A perfect copy, uncut, with the first title-page and the rare leaf of errata was truly as the music of the spheres to him, and this wholly irrespective of the fact that it meant a thousand dollars profit. And yet I have heard him deliver a volley of titanic passion upon an erring binder who had exceeded his estimate by seventy-five cents. He had the strange inconsequence of all great men, and that he was a great man in his own sphere I had no doubt from the moment I set eyes upon him.

He was clearly working at a deadly pace, though one did not suppose that so vital an instrument could die. More than once I insisted that he must come out to lunch when he proposed to work straight through the day without respite. And then he would come docilely, with a rare and childlike charm. He was so accustomed to command (I always thrill at the thought of his domination in the great London sale rooms) that he liked to be mastered in some of the simple affairs of living. It was the stuff of comedy to see him buttoning up his overcoat, saying the while that he couldn't spare the time, and that if he went out there was no one else . . .

He had the charming courtesy that so often marks the tyrant. To call on him after shop hours would sometimes be to find him readier for relaxation. Then Mrs. Smith must be found: we must all have dinner together, and a theatre—any theatre we liked—afterward. And when it came, what a dinner! A thing to make the most practised hostess in two capitals envious, arranged and carried through with the satisfaction of a successful schoolboy on holiday. I shall never forget him at a certain hotel on that occasion. He shone with power, the rare power of making his friends happy. And I remember, too, a heroic evening with Dr. Rosenbach and Mitchell Kennerley and Lewis Hind, when he helped to make bibliography a theme worthy of an Odyssey; while I, who like to put a pencil note in my first edition of Boswell's Johnson that it is " rare," and in the case, say, of the 1646 Shirley, to add " extremely," listened to him and his peer of Philadelphia defining what " rare " meant to them. Nothing was admitted of which there were known more than two copies and a half.

G. D. S'.s generosity was in keeping with the general build of the man. Whenever I got a chance I attended the Anderson sales, and took a place beside him. His bidding was full of humour. He would carry a book freely by twenty dollar bids, speaking by a flick of his catalogue, and then well on in the hundreds he would make an advance of twenty-five cents, delight-

ing naïvely to tumble the auctioneer in his stride.
New York has many great booksellers, and they, Dr.
" Rosey " and others, could keep the wits even of
G. D. S. alive; but Mr. Drake and Mr. Wells and
Mr. North would, I am sure, gladly allow that he was
the man who really set the pace. And sometimes,
when he was insistent on one lot after another, the
competition would flag a little, and some scarce
book would slip through at a notably bargain price.
Then his generosity showed itself.   Once a beautiful
copy of a very rare seventeenth-century poet in his first
edition was up.   There was a lull in the bidding, and it
went to G. D. S. at a considerable sum, but at about
one-third of its current market price.   Although
sometimes I asked him to bid for me on commission,
I had not done so in this case, considering the book
to be altogether beyond my reach.   As it was knocked
down to him, he turned to me and said, " You can
have it if you like."   He could have made five hundred
dollars profit on it within twenty-four hours.   That
was a big thing to do, really a big thing of the spirit.
Don Quixote would have done it.

Two days before I left America, I dragged him out
to lunch as was our custom.   He was coming to England
soon.   He had a colt that might be good enough for
the Derby.   He would christen it John Drinkwater.
He had just bought a French library for a quarter of
a million dollars.   Would I write a preface for Miss
Henrietta Bartlett's lectures ?   He was to publish them.
I selected a Cowper letter from his stock.   He called

for his cashier to make the bill out. The cashier was not in: "Cut it out, then—take it to England with my love, Drinkwater." We walked down the street together, and took photographs. Then on the morning that we were sailing I ran across to say good-bye. He was always up and about soon after six o'clock. I made one last plunge among his books, and he came back to the hotel for breakfast. He would be in England before the summer was out, and of course we should meet. And when next I came to America I was to live at his country house. There would be motor-cars, and he liked the country, to sit and look at the pigs. "Go on buying books, my boy; you buy right, and you can't go wrong with them." On the ship I found my cabin garlanded with the hospitality in which America leaves every other people standing. And among the piled tributes of friendship, colossal among them was the hamper of fruit and flowers from G. D. S. With some people such magnitude is mere ostentation. With others it is native largeness of heart. From him it was a splendid buoyancy, a determination to outdo all. We sailed, and two days later a Marconigram came. G. D. S. was dead. I have never suffered so dark a sorrow for a friend of so short a knowing.

SOME LETTERS FROM MATTHEW ARNOLD TO ROBERT BROWNING

SOME LETTERS FROM MATTHEW ARNOLD
TO ROBERT BROWNING

THERE recently came into my possession a packet of letters written by Matthew Arnold to Robert Browning. That some correspondence should never be published is clear. Nothing, for example, can ever justify the publication of Keats's love letters to Fanny Brawne. Such letters were not only written in the strictest privacy of emotion, but they were, further, written in a manner that could only be understood by the person to whom they were addressed. Any judgment of Keats's character formed from these letters is a judgment which no one in the world has any right to make, since the evidence is neither admissible nor intelligible. Even Matthew Arnold, the most fastidious of critics and the most lucid judge of character, allowed himself in spite of his protests to be misled into such a judgment, and his estimate of Keats suffers in the process. But, with such exceptions, a man's correspondence will often, even when it is upon inconsiderable affairs, add a particular charm to the figure presented by his work. Cowper and Gray and FitzGerald would have suffered some loss of their due fame had their letters never been published to the world. The present little series of letters, trifling in occasion for the most part, show both the poets concerned in a very pleasing and friendly light, and it is for this reason that, with Lady Sandhurst's permission, I now publish them.

The relations between Browning and Arnold seem always to have been extremely cordial. They exchanged books, generally with inscriptions of the warmest regard. In Arnold's pocket diary* for 1845 there is a note of books " to be read from October 1845 ———." The first entry is Glanvil's *Vanity of Dogmatising*. A little boasting in these things is pardonable, and I like to provoke the collector's envy by saying that I am the happy possessor of Arnold's own copy of Glanvil† that was to be immortalized in the line " and near me on the grass lies Glanvil's book." The volume contains Arnold's bookplate, and on the fly-leaf in his writing, " E lib.: M. Arnold. 1844." But to add to the delight, this is followed by a further inscription, also in Arnold's hand, " Given by M. Arnold to R. Browning. Augt. 5th, 1879." But even that is not all. Lower down on the same page is yet another note, this time in Browning's writing, which runs thus: " (It contains the story which suggested to M. Arnold his exquisite poem *The Gypsey-*

* One of three in my possession, unpublished, and containing a good deal of amusing information to which I hope to return.

† The title-page in full is as follows: " The Vanity of/Dogmatising: /or/Confidence in Opinions./Manifested in a/Discourse/of the/ Shortness and Uncertainty/of our/Knowledge,/And its Causes;/With some/Reflexions on Peripateticism;/and/An Apology for Philosophy./ By Jos. Glanvill, M.A./London, Printed by E. C. for Henry Eversden at the Grey-/Hound in St. Pauls Church Yard. 1661."

Scholar, R. B.)"* The leaf is a charming note upon the relations between the two poets.. In 1881 Arnold sends Browning a copy of his Byron selection " With affectionate regard. M. A.," an inscription to which Browning adds his own name and the date " June 25. 81." And doubtless there are existent many other examples of like courtesies. Of Browning's gifts to Arnold in this kind there are two records in the letters here printed.

In 1870 Browning, writing to Miss Isa Blagden, makes this touching reference:

". . . Florence would be irritating, and, on the whole, insufferable—Yet I never hear of anyone going thither but my heart is twitched. There is a good, charming, little singing German lady, Miss Regan, who told me the other day that she was just about revisiting her aunt, Madame Sabatier, who you may know, or know of—and I felt as if I should immensely like to glide, for a long summer-day through the streets and between the old stone-walls,—unseen come and unseen go—perhaps by some miracle, I shall do so—and look up at Villa Brichieri as Arnold's Gypsy-Scholar gave one wistful look at ' the line of festal light in Christ Church Hall,' before he went to sleep in some forgotten grange. . . ."

Seven years later, in telling another correspondent of a recent visit to Oxford where he had been Jowett's guest in the company of the Archbishop of Canterbury, the Bishop of London, Lord Coleridge, Lord Lansdowne, and other notabilities, he says:

* Browning's version of Arnold's title is not uncharacteristic.

" . . . dinner done, speechifying set in vigorously.
. . . Mr. Green (drank) to Literature and Science
delivering a most undeserved eulogium on myself,
with a more rightly directed one on Arnold, Swinburne, and the old pride of Balliol, Clough: this was
cleverly and almost touchingly answered by dear Mat
Arnold. . . ."

Arnold's personal affection for Browning, who was
ten years his senior, is clearly written in these letters,
and Mrs. Arnold writing to Browning thanking him
for " words of sympathy " written on Arnold's death
in 1888, says: " He had the most warm affection, admiration and respect for you, and I like to
think how much he would have valued and how
deeply he would have been touched by all you say
of him."

I have, so far as I could, added to the letters such
notes as seemed necessary for their explanation.
This doubtless unimportant task has not been made
any easier by the fact that the beautiful collection of
Arnold's letters edited by Mr. G. W. E. Russell in
1895 contains no index.

Letter I.

[Addressed to Browning at 1, Chichester Road,
Upper Westbourne Terrace. Arnold had moved to
Chester Square in 1858. At the date of this letter he
was thirty-nine years of age, and Browning forty-nine.
Browning had recently returned to England after

Mrs. Browning's death, which took place in Florence on June 30, 1861.

The Madame du Quaire was Fanny du Quaire, the sister of John F. Blackett, the member for Newcastle. She was already an old friend of Browning's, and a sympathetic reader and critic of both poets. Arnold, writing to her in 1858 of *Merope*, says: " Make Browning look at it if he is in Florence; one of the very best antique fragments I know is a fragment of a *Hippolytus* by him." This would be the *Artemis Prologizes* which was published in the third number of *Bells and Pome-granates* in 1842, and is referred to by Arnold in Letter XIII. In 1861 Arnold quotes Madame du Quaire to his mother as praising his poem *A Southern Night.*

Writing to his mother on November 13, 1861, Arnold says: " We had a pleasant dinner-party the other night. Froude I always find attractive, though I think he has very sinister ways of looking at history." From the fact that Browning was not mentioned the inference is that he was not able to accept the invitation.]

" My dear Mr. Browning,—Will you give us the pleasure of your company at dinner next Thursday, the 7th, at ¼ past 7 ? You will meet Mme. du Quaire, and, I hope, Froude. •

" Most truly yours,
" M. Arnold.

" 2 Chester Square,
  " *Novber* 4*th,* 1861."

LETTER II.

[This and all the subsequent letters are addressed to 19, Warwick Crescent. I have found nothing to show whether Browning went or not.]

" 2 CHESTER SQUARE,
" *Nov^{ber} 6th* [1862].

" DEAR MR. BROWNING,—If you are in town and disengaged will you give Mrs. Arnold and me the pleasure of your company at dinner on Sunday (the 9th) at ¼ past 7, to meet Mme. du Quaire ?   She goes out of town on Monday.
" Believe me,
" Sincerely yours,
" MATTHEW ARNOLD."

LETTER III.

[The teacher, as we gather from Letter IX., was for Arnold's eldest son, Thomas, and was duly engaged.]

" THE ATHENAEUM,
" *Oct^{ber}* 18th, 1864.

" MY DEAR BROWNING,—If you are back in London will you kindly send me the name and address of the German you mentioned to me as a teacher of music for my little boy.   Or, if you would mention the case to him, and send him to call at my house at any time he can make convenient, letting me know what time is fixed, perhaps that would be the best plan.   My little boy is full of ardour to begin.
" Ever sincerely yours,
" MATTHEW ARNOLD.

" 2 CHESTER SQUARE."

Letter IV.

[Sir George Bowyer, Bart., was an eminent lawyer and jurisprudent. There is no trace, so far as I can discover, of what Browning wanted, but as he was now writing *The Ring and the Book*, of which he tells us in 1862 that he " had the whole story pretty well in his head," although the first volume was not published till 1868, the questions may possibly have had some reference to the machinery of that poem.]

" The Athenaeum,
" Dec^{ber} 19th, 1864.

" My dear Browning,—Every day I have been hoping to see you here, but not having that pleasure I write to say that I have spoken to Henry Bowyer about your wish to ask some questions of his brother: and any morning you like to call on Sir George Bowyer at his chambers in the Temple, he will be happy to see you.

" Ever sincerely yours,
" Matthew Arnold."

Letter V.

[Joseph Milsand had been a friend of Browning's from 1852, and the 1863 reprint of *Sordello* was dedicated to him, and the *Parleyings with Certain People*, 1887, was inscribed to his memory a year after his death. In April, 1865, Arnold writes to his wife from Paris: " On Tuesday I dined with Milsand, one of the *Revue des deux Mondes* set." Milsand published in 1864 a brochure on Ruskin, and this is probably the volume referred to. Why Arnold's confidence in Browning had caused him to disregard " one or two occasions of reading the book," I cannot say. If the notice was written it does not seem to have been collected.]

" THE ATHENAEUM,
" *Feb^y* 17th, 1865.

" MY DEAR BROWNING,—Many thanks for Milsand's book: I had that confidence in you, that I disregarded one or two occasions of reading the book, though it looked interesting and Palgrave gave the highest report of it. I have promised (for my sins) to do two things for a newspaper; and I shall try and make a notice of this book one of them.

" Ever sincerely yours,
" MATTHEW ARNOLD."

LETTER VI.

[De Circourt was a Parisian friend of Arnold's. Again there is no evidence as to whether Browning went or not.]

" 2 CHESTER SQUARE,
" *April* 5th [1866].

" MY DEAR BROWNING,—I hope you will be able to give us the pleasure of your company at dinner next Tuesday, the 10th, at ¼ to 8. You will meet M. de Circourt, whom I think you know. He has only just come to town from Yorkshire, and he goes back to Paris on Wednesday: that is why I give you such improperly short notice.

" Ever most sincerely yours,
" MATTHEW ARNOLD."

LETTER VII.

[Three days after the date of this letter, on November 9, Arnold writes to his mother: "We had a very pleasant dinner-party last night which grew up out of small beginnings. First, I had asked Lake to dine quite alone with us, then a M. Milsand, a Frenchman and a remarkable writer, who had been very civil to me when I was in Paris last year, called unexpectedly, and I added him to Lake; then I found Milsand was staying with Browning, and I added Browning; then Lord Houghton went with me and William Forster to Spurgeon's lecture, and, having asked William of course to dine if he stayed in London, I found that Lord Houghton was a friend of Milsand's, and so I asked him too; then Flu suggested that we ought to ask the Custs, which was very true, so we asked them; and they all came. This is how one's resolutions of having no more dinner-parties get set aside."]

" Nov^ber 6th [1866].

" MY DEAR BROWNING,—Mr. Milsand is coming to dine with us quite quietly on Thursday at ¼ past 7 (a real ½ past), and I hope and trust you will be able to give us the pleasure of your company too. It is an age since I have seen you.

" Ever most sincerely,
" MATTHEW ARNOLD.

" 2 CHESTER SQUARE."

Letter VIII.

[This was just before Arnold moved from Chester Square to Harrow. Mr. Robert Cust kindly informs me that the Captain Cust referred to was his uncle, Major (then Captain) Henry Cust, who married Mrs. Streatfield. Barley (a pet name) Streatfield was this lady's daughter.]

"Athenaeum Club
"(2 Chester Square),
"*Feb* 24*th*, 1868.

"My dear Browning,—I should like to get you once more within my house before I leave it: if you are by chance still disengaged for next Saturday, will you come and dine with us that day at ½ past 7 ? You will meet no one but Fanny du Quaire and Barley Streatfield and Capt. Cust, for we are still living shut up, but Mrs. Arnold will be as glad as I shall if you can come to us thus quietly.

"Believe me,
"ever sincerely yours,
"Matthew Arnold."

Letter IX.

[Arnold's eldest son, Thomas, died at Harrow on November 23, at the age of sixteen. The volume referred to was presumably one of the first two of *The Ring and the Book*, which were published in the winter months of this year. It is to be hoped that it beguiled the tedium of the examination room. Arnold's educational duties were now a pretty desperate business, and he had to take precautions against being swamped by them, and in a letter to his mother, written in this month, he says: " I divide my papers (second year grammar) through every day, taking in Christmas Day, Saturdays, and Sundays. In this way I bring them down to twenty-five a day, which I can do without the strain on my head and eyes which forty a day, or—as I used often to make it in old times by delaying at first—eighty or ninety a day would be."]

" Harrow,
" Dec^{ber} 5th, 1868.

" My dear Browning,—We have lately had a great loss—our dear invalid boy for whom you helped us to a singing-master; we had kept him sixteen years in spite of everybody prophesying that we should not rear him, and having kept him so long does not make it easier to part with him now. Letters and parcels have been accumulating and I have only just opened your volume with its kind—too kind—inscription. The poem looks most interesting, and it will rouse me and bring me back to life as few other things could. I shall busy myself with it all this next week while I have to sit presiding at a long weary examination which will have now this merit at least that it will give me time and quiet for your poetry.

" With the most sincere thanks,
" ever yours,
" Matthew Arnold."

Letter X.

[Arnold's second son, Trevenen William, had died at Harrow a few days before, at the age of eighteen.]

"Harrow,
"*Wednesday* [*Feb.* 21*st*, 1872].

"My dear Browning,—Thank you for your most kind note. It always gives me pleasure to think of you, and to know that I have your kind thoughts. These poor children whom we call only children after the flesh—how much nearer and dearer they are to us than any others!

"Ever yours affect^ly,
"Matthew Arnold."

Letter XI.

[The volume referred to was no doubt *Aristophanes' Apology*, published in 1875. The *Inn Album* was also published in the same year, but did not appear until November.]

"Athenaeum Club,
"*May* 20*th*, 1875.

"My dear Browning,—Many thanks for your poem which I shall keep to read when my summer holiday comes and I can read a poem steadily. It is sure to leave me with the impression which your writings from the first have given me and which the writings of so few other living people give me—that the author is what the French well call a *grand esprit*.

"Sincerely yours,
"Matthew Arnold."

Letter XII.

[Arnold had moved from Harrow to Cobham in 1873. This letter and the next one brings to light, so far as I am aware for the first time, a charming passage between the two poets. Browning seems already to have been approached by St. Andrews some years earlier to see whether he would take office in succession to John Stuart Mill. He declined as he did again now. Browning does not seem to have written directly to *The Times*, but the following extracts from that paper in connexion with the matter tell an interesting little story of their own.

November 7th, 1877.

"St. Andrews, *Nov.* 6.

A meeting of the party who were supporting the Marquis of Salisbury for the Rectorial Chair was held to-night, when it was unanimously agreed to bring forward Mr. Matthew Arnold in opposition to Mr. Robert Browning, seeing that the Marquis had declined to allow himself to be nominated. The poll is fixed for the 22nd inst.

November 15, 1877.

"St. Andrews, *Nov.* 14.

A meeting for the nomination of candidates for the Rectorship was held last night. It was stated that Mr. Matthew Arnold had written declining to stand in opposition to Mr. Robert Browning, and that in consequence his nomination would not be persevered with. Mr. Robert Browning was then duly nominated, and it is most probable that he will now be elected without opposition. The election is fixed for the 22nd inst.

November 19, 1877.
                                    " St. Andrews, *Nov.* 18.

The Conservative students of the University have
resolved to nominate the Right Hon. Robert Lowe
for the Rectorial Chair in opposition to Mr. Robert
Browning, the poet.   The supporters of the latter are,
however, particularly strong, and are confident they
will carry their man against any candidate that may
now be proposed.

November 21, 1877.
                                    " St. Andrews, *Nov.* 19.

The Right Hon. Robert Lowe was nominated to-day
for the Rectorship of the University, in opposition
to Mr. Browning, the poet.   Since then, however,
intelligence having been received that Mr. Browning
declines to be a candidate, a large section of the students
are anxious to support Mr. Matthew Arnold, who at
a former stage of the contest retired in favour of
Mr. Browning; but it is doubtful if the former gentleman will allow his name to be again brought forward.
The poll will be taken on Thursday.

November 22, 1877.
                                    " St. Andrews, *Nov.* 21.

Both Mr. Robert Browning and Mr. Matthew
Arnold declining to stand for the office of Rector, it
was unanimously agreed at a meeting held yesterday
to elect Professor Tyndall. . . .

November 23, 1877.
                                    " St. Andrews, *Nov.* 22.

The triennial election of a Rector for the University
of St. Andrews, in the room of the Dean of West-

minster, was held this afternoon. The election has been remarkable for the number of gentlemen mentioned in connexion with the office and the difficulty experienced by the students in inducing any of them to be nominated. Mr. Robert Browning was for a time the popular candidate, and his return would easily have been secured had he not withdrawn. Mr. Matthew Arnold and Professor Tyndall would also have been carried had they stood; but a negative reply being received from both of them, the students, as late as Wednesday afternoon, were without a candidate. A mass meeting held late in the evening selected Lord Selborne and the Right Hon. Gathorne Hardy, and the election was thus at the close resolved into a political contest. . . .]

> " PAINS HILL COTTAGE,
> " COBHAM, SURREY,
> " Nov^{ber} 7th, 1877.

" MY DEAR BROWNING,—I have just seen in *The Times* that the St. Andrews students who were supporting Ld. Salisbury propose now to bring me forward in opposition to you. I should not allow myself to be brought forward in any case, because I am a schoolinspector;—but I hope I need hardly add that least of all should I allow myself to be brought forward in opposition to *you*.

> " Believe me,
> " Cordially yours,
> " MATTHEW ARNOLD.

" *P.S.*—I have heard nothing from St. Andrews; if I hear, or indeed whether I hear or not, I shall say what I have said to you."

LETTER XIII.

[*The Agamemnon of Aeschylus, Transcribed by Robert Browning,* was published in 1877, Browning claiming in his preface that " the poorest translation provided only it be faithful . . . will not only suffice to display what an eloquent friend maintains to be the all in all of poetry—' the action of the piece,' " and going on to appeal to a celebrated passage from Arnold's *Preface* of 1853.]

" PAINS HILL COTTAGE,
" COBHAM, SURREY,
" *Nov*^{ber} 26*th,* 1877.

" MY DEAR BROWNING,—I cannot help thinking that in a packet of some half-dozen letters, which was sent after me into Suffolk where I was on a visit, was a letter from you. The packet has been lost: I have been waiting and waiting in hopes of recovering it, but without result. Probably you told me of your intention not to stand for the Rectorship of St. Andrews; as it was, your letter in *The Times* took me quite by surprise. I wish you had let them elect you; a Lord Rector has not to make a speech—your detestation, I know—he has only to write and read an address. And an address from you would have been full of interest. However, it is not to be; and my ignorance of your intentions made no difference as to my coming forward, as I have determined never to come forward for a post of this kind while I am a school-inspector; of course, whether I had been a school-inspector or not, my allowing myself to be brought forward against *you* was out of the question.

" I am very glad to have the ' Agamemnon ' from you, and thank you much for sending it. I will not deny that I prefer your manner in *Artemis Prologizes:* but I can truly say of the present work, that, given a certain problem which you had fixed for yourself in dealing with Aeschylus, I am filled with admiration of the vigour and ability which you show in grappling with it.

"Believe me,
"Most sincerely yours,
"MATTHEW ARNOLD."

LETTER XIV.

[Arnold was still living at Cobham; but he took first No. 3, then No. 1, Eccleston Square, furnished, for a season. Grant Duff was Sir Mountstuart Grant Duff. He was appointed Under-Secretary of State for India in Mr. Gladstone's first Administration and was afterwards Governor of Madras. Again there is nothing to show whether Browning went.]

"1 ECCLESTON SQUARE, S.W.,
"*March 27th* [1878].

"MY DEAR BROWNING,—Could you dine with us next Tuesday, the 2nd of April, at ¼ to 8? I would gladly have given you more notice, but I want to catch Grant Duff before he starts for Algiers.

"Most sincerely yours,
"MATTHEW ARNOLD."

Here the series ends. Arnold lived ten years longer, Browning twelve. That the affectionate intimacy was never broken is clear from Mrs. Arnold's letter that has been quoted. And that the friendship continued to be a treasured one in the Arnold family until Browning's own death is shown by a further letter from Mrs. Arnold written to Browning when he was seventy-seven years of age, a few months only before he died, asking him if he could be present at her daughter's wedding, not only for her own gratification, but because his coming would have touched and pleased his old friend. Mrs. Arnold concludes, " I hope, dear Mr. Browning, you will not mind my asking you in this way, and of course I shall quite understand if you cannot come. But the remembrance of old days has been strong upon me so I cannot help writing." And so closes a little chapter of literary biography, inconsiderable perhaps, but in its example of courtesy not without something of Arnold's own favourite " sweetness and light."

SOME UNPUBLISHED LETTERS

SHENSTONE AT THE LEASOWES

["A MAN of most elegant genius; remarkable for the utmost tenderness and sweetness of his poetical composition; extremely fond of ease and retirement." Thus, quoting from the Latin, wrote a friend when William Shenstone died in 1763. His poetical composition probably finds few readers nowadays, though Mr. Iola Williams and other eighteenth-century enthusiasts have brought him forward a little again of late. Sir Arthur Quiller Couch could not find a corner for him in the *Oxford Book of English Verse*. And yet Shenstone has always been a name, and when we return to his verses we find, as is usually the case, that this has not been for nothing. My own favourite is *Slender's Ghost*; no recent anthologist seems to have chosen it, so I will give myself the pleasure of printing it here.

SLENDER'S GHOST.

Beneath a church-yard yew,
　Decay'd and worn with age,
At dusk of eve methought I spy'd
Poor Slender's ghost, that whimp'ring cry'd,
　O sweet O sweet Anne Page !

Ye gentle bards ! give ear !
　Who talk of amorous rage,
Who spoil the lilly, rob the rose,
Come learn of me to weep your woes:
　O sweet O sweet Anne Page !

Why shou'd such labour'd strains
　　Your formal muse engage?
I never dreamt of flame or dart,
That fir'd my breast, or pierc'd my heart,
　　But sigh'd, O sweet Anne Page!

And you! whose love sick minds
　　No med'cine can assuage!
Accuse the leech's art no more,
But learn of Slender to deplore;
　　O sweet O sweet Anne Page!

And ye! whose souls are held,
　　Like linnets in a cage!
Who talk of fetters, links, and chains,
Attend, and imitate my strains!
　　O sweet O sweet Anne Page!

And you who boast or grieve,
　　What horrid wars ye wage!
Of wounds receiv'd from many an eye;
Yet mean as I do, when I sigh
　　O sweet O sweet Anne Page!

Hence ev'ry fond conceit
　　Of shepherd or of sage!
'Tis Slender's voice, 'tis Slender's way
Expresses all you have to say,
　　O sweet O sweet Anne Page!

About Shenstone's extreme fondness for ease and retirement at least there can be no question. Educated at Solihull, near Birmingham, and at Pembroke College, Oxford, he formed two or three friendships at the University that lasted through his life, and were among the most important circumstances of it. Chief of these were Richard Jago, the poet of *Edgehill*, with whom he had also been at school, Anthony Whistler, and Richard Graves, also poets.   The last of these became Shenstone's biographer, and relates how he first met the poet.   On going to Oxford at the age of seventeen, he was asked to join a club where they read Greek and drank water of an evening—water-drinking just then having been brought into great vogue by the vegetarian Dr. Cheyne.   Graves, however, was shortly " seduced from this mortifying symposium " by another society where they drank ale and smoked tobacco and made puns and sang bacchanalian catches.   A little later still, and he left this for yet another company that rose to port wine and arrack-punch.   And, lastly, he was sometimes with " a sort of flying squadron of plain, sensible, matter-of-fact men," confined to no club.   In each of these galleys, except the water-drinking one, he met Shenstone and Whistler, and after a time they started an informal club of their own, meeting most evenings for reading.

Soon after leaving Oxford, Shenstone by inheritance took possession of The Leasowes, the house at Halesowen that became no less famous than his poetry. On a small income, that he had no disposition to augment, he lived frugally, wrote his verses, cultivated the art of landscape gardening with a success that attracted the attention of the fashionable world, and wrote lots of letters, Jago and Graves being his principal correspondents, until he died at the age of sixty.   These letters are far better than is commonly known; they have something of Cowper's quality, and, indeed, there was not a little in common between these poets, both in character and habit. The following letter, from editorial marks on it, was intended for publication in Dodsley's edition of 1769, but for some reason it was not included, and, so far as I can trace, is now printed for the first time. It was after a visit to Whistler in Oxfordshire, that had ended in Shenstone leaving in a huff, that the poet on staying the first night of his return journey at Edgehill wrote:

> Whoe'er has travell'd life's dull round,
>   Where'er his stages may have been,
> May sigh to think he still has found
>   The warmest welcome at an inn.

The rest of the poem, *Written at an Inn at Henley*, came afterwards, and far less successfully. The quarrel was made up, and when four years later Whistler died, Shenstone wrote to Graves, " Poor Mr. Whistler ! not a single acquaintance have I made, not a single picture or curiosity have I purchased; not a single embellishment have I given to my place, since he was last here, but I have had his approbation and his amusement in my eye. I will assuredly inscribe my larger urn to his memory; nor shall I pass it without a pleasing melancholy during the remainder of my days."

Of Ferdinand, Lord Dudley I know only that Mr. Graves—the Revd. Mr., being rector of Claverton for over fifty years—says that his rank and title made him of some consequence, " though he was so unfortunate as not to have had an education suitable to them," and of his lordship's sister and her Mr. Jorden I know less. Nor does Sir Thomas Head convey anything to me—just Sir Thomas Head in a Shenstone letter, which, after all, is something. The letter is undated, but it clearly is from Leasowes.]

" DEAR SIR,
        " I did indeed give you up for lost, as a correspondent, & find by your letter that I am to expect but very few future ones. I will endeavour all I can to avoid any suspicion of your indifference to my own satisfaction but I don't know for certain that I shall be able, unless you assist my Endeavours, like my good Genius, by a course of suitable Epistles · at certain distances—I myself correspond but very little now, so you will meet with the more Indulgence—I don't find by your letter that you have much more Philosophy than me. I can't tell indeed what the situation of y^r House is, I own mine gives me offence on no other consideration than that it does not receive a sufficient Number of polite Friends, or that it is not fit to receive 'em, were they so dispos'd. I wou'd else cultivate an Acquaintance with about Three or Four in my Neighbourhood, that are of a Degree of Elegance, & station superior to the common Run. But I make it a certain Rule Arcere profanu vulgus. Persons of vulgar *Minds,* who will despise you for the want of a good set of Chairs, or an uncouth Fire-shovel at the same time that they can't taste any Excellence in a mind that overlooks those things; or, (To make a conceit of this Sentiment) with whom 'tis in vain that y^r Mind is furnish'd if y^r walls are naked—Indeed one loses much of one's Acquisitions in virtue by an Hour's converse

with such as Judge of merit by Money. Yet I am now
& then impell'd by the social Passion to sit half an Hour
in my Kitchen.

" I was all along an Admirer of Sʳ Thomas Head's
Humour & Wit, And I beg you wou'd represent me in
that Light if occasion happens. 'Tis not impossible
that I may penetrate this winter as far as yʳ neighbourhood, connecting a set of visits which I have in my
Eye—Tell Mr. Whistler when you see him that if
he must have *some* Distemper, I cannot but be pleased
that it is one which is a Forerunner of Longevity—
Don't tell him so neither for the compliment is
trite.

" From the *Birmingham Gazette*—' We hear that on
Thursday last was married at Hales-owen in Shrop-
shire Mʳ Jorden an eminent Gunsmith of this Town
to a sister of the Rᵗ Honᵇˡᵉ Ferdinand Lᵈ Dudley.'
I was yesterday at the Grange, where his old Father
(with a number of People) was celebrating the nuptials
of his Son; when in the midst of his Feasting, high
Jollity and grand Alliance the old Fellow bethought
him of a Piece of Timber in the neighbourhood that
was convertible into good Gunsticks, & had some of it
sent for into the Room by way of Specimen! Animæ
nil magna laudis egentis!

" Pray is yʳ Sister at Smethwick?—for I have not
heard. You said you wou'd give me yʳ Picture which
I long earnestly for cou'dn't you contrive to have it
sent me directly? I am quite in your Debt with
regard to downright goods & moveables & what is
the proper subject of an Inventory—neque in pessima
munerū ferres divite me scilicet astrum quas aut
Parrhasius prohibit aut scopas—sed non hæc mihi vis!
I will however endeavour to be more upon a Par with
you wᵗʰ regard to presents, tho' I never can with

regard to the Pleasures I have receiv'd frō y^r conversation—I make People wonder at my Exploits in pulling down walls, Hovels, Cow-houses etc.: and my Place is not the same.   I am that is, wth regard to you a Faithfull Friend, & h^{ble} Servt,

" W. S.

" Mr Whistler & you & I & Sr T. Head (who I shou'd name first, speaking after the manner of Men) have just variety enough & not too much, in our Charact: to make an Interview whenever it happens Entertaining—I mean tho' we were not old Friends & Acquaintance."

MR. BEATTIE WOULD LIKE SEVENTY
POUNDS

[THE poet of *The Minstrel* is, perhaps, not now much remembered. But he was a considerable figure in his time; how much of a figure can perhaps best be seen in the beautiful symbolical portrait by Reynolds that adorns the Senate Room in the University of Aberdeen, where James Beattie was at one time Professor of Moral Philosophy and Logic. He was born in 1735, so that the following letter was written when he was forty-seven. It is addressed to " William Strahan Esquire, Member of Parliament, London." Strahan, at that time member for Wootton-Bassett, was the publisher who had been in partnership with the more celebrated Andrew Millar, and had then joined Thomas Cadell, to whom reference is made in the letter. Strahan was later responsible for the publication of Dr. Johnson's *Prayers and Meditations*, and incurred Beattie's censure for not " retrenching occasionally a few things, which throw in some degree a ridicule on a work of so serious a nature, and which, by giving cause for scoffing, will perhaps diminish the good effects the book might otherwise be expected to produce: had he likewise substituted Elizabeth (which Boswell tells me was Mrs. Johnson's real name) in the place of such a ridiculous appellation as ' Tetty,' surely no man could have found fault with' the change." Shocking as this must be to Johnsonians, even they will be touched by Beattie's gentle appeal for £70.

The book referred to in the first paragraph is the *Dissertations on Memory and Imagination, Dreaming . . . etc.*, which was published in 1783. On January 30 in this year, Beattie wrote to Mrs. Montagu: " My new book has been in the press for some time and I have now received sixteen sheets of it, which is about one-fifth of the whole. It is a quarto of the same size nearly with my last, and from what I have seen is very correctly printed. The proprietor, Mr. Strahan, thinks it will be ready for publication in the spring. I am afraid the plainness and simplicity in the style will not hit the taste of the present race of orators and critics; who seem to think that the old English tongue, and the old English constitution, stand equally in need of change. . . . My models of English are Addison, and those who write like Addison, particularly yourself, Madam, and Lord Lyttelton. . . ." Dr. Rose is presumably the William Rose who, like Beattie himself, had been educated at Marischal College, Aberdeen, and afterwards became a schoolmaster in London.

Sir William Forbes, Beattie's biographer, does not include this letter in his two volumes of 1806, and it does not seem to have been printed elsewhere.]

" Aberdeen,
" Dear Sir,   " 3 *December*, 1782.
    " I wrote about six weeks ago in answer to your obliging favour of the 10 October, which inclosed the first sheet of my book; the type, the paper, and the

correctness whereof are all entirely to my mind. I
wish a copy of each sheet, as it comes corrected from
the press, could be sent me in franks; that I may have
time to give a leisurely perusal to the whole, before
publication.

" I did not think, that I should have occasion to
touch any of the copy-money for some time: and so I
think I wrote to Dr. Rose.   But I am just now in want
of seventy pounds, and should be very much obliged
to you and Mr. Cadel, if you could make me a re-
mittance to that amount.   But if this be inconvenient,
or if there be any standing rule which forbids the payment of copy-money till after the book is published,
it is no great matter: as I can without difficulty borrow
that sum.

" Our apprehensions of famine are not so great as
when I wrote last, at least in this part of the country.
The crop is got in in many parts; and many judicious
farmers are of opinion that it is not a very bad one.
There is a great stock of cattle in the country, and no
deficiency of fodder; and we daily look for some vessels
with grain, from Norfolk and Lincolnshire.   In this
town we have subscribed £2,000, to be laid out in
premiums for encouraging the importation of grain.
So that our prospects begin to brighten, and the
people are recovering their spirits.   Yet in the inland
and highland parts of the country there must be great
scarcity.

" I beg my best comp^{ts} to Dr. Rose.   I owe him
a letter, and will pay it soon.   I am, with the utmost
regard, Dear Sir, Your most affectionate humble serv^t·

" J. BEATTIE.

" WILLIAM STRAHAN, ESQRE."

GEORGE CRABBE AT SEVENTY-FOUR

[IN his later life Crabbe was frequently the guest of Mr. Samuel Hoare at his house on Hampstead Heath. It was from here that the poet, then aged seventy-four, wrote the following letter. His correspondent was, no doubt, a member of the Waldron family who were among his most friendly parishioners at Trowbridge in Wiltshire, where he was rector at the time. But I hope that this Miss Waldron may have had something to do with the " Miss Waldron, late of Tamworth," whom Crabbe met in 1791 at Beccles, where " four or five spinsters of independent fortune had formed a sort of Protestant nunnery." One of these was, according to the poet's son George, " dear, good-humoured, hearty, masculine Miss Waldron, who could sing a jovial song like a fox-hunter, and like him I had almost said toss a glass. . . . When we took our morning rides, she generally drove my father in *her* phaeton, and interested him exceedingly by her strong understanding and conversational powers." John was the " John Crabbe, so long the affectionate and un-wearied assistant of his father in his latter days," as we learn from the younger George's life of the poet. I regret that I can throw no light on the difference with Mrs. Everett, or on the identity of that lady. Hatchard, the bookseller of Piccadilly, was at one time

Crabbe's publisher. "The Strange Gentleman," like Mrs. Everett, eludes me.]

"HAMPSTEAD,
"10 *July*, 1828.

"My dear Miss Waldron

"Though I trust that my Son mentions my Enquiries respecting your Health and my Hopes of hearing a chearful Account, yet I cannot be satisfied without addressing my Question immediately to yourself—Are you well? and if you cannot say so much, are you in the way to be well? do you gain Strength and Freedom from Pain, if not daily or weekly yet on the whole? I shall rejoice to learn this and shall think of meeting you with great Comfort. I have a rather severe Return of my Pain and take Steel at this Time, with the same Trust in it, as Success has taught me to have.

"Of my Adventures and Excursions I will relate nothing till my Return and then I shall have so little to communicate that I shall be rather a Hearer than a Speaker and that best suits me for I never could speak in my Life to any good Purpose, but I am a good Hearer and have one tolerable Ear at my Friend's Service and especially a Friend who knows and trusts me, for Hearer as I profess myself to be, I would not willingly yield that One Ear to those who say to me, nothing more than to Every one beside.

"You have heard me speak so often of my Friends here that I have nothing new to relate of them: why they are so kind and good to me as they continue to be, I protest to you, I cannot tell. I am of no more use than a Log upon the Water, floating about as the Tide serves, but doing nothing & I should think oftentimes in the way, but still treated as if I gave as much Pleasure to them as I receive myself.

"I want to know if you be at Home and who is

with you for John tells me nothing of that kind: no
Particulars.   Mrs Everett I conclude has left you:
I am afraid I never succeeded in my Attempts to regain
the Favour of the Lady and that is hard for I tried
repeatedly and thought at one time I had succeeded
but I resigned the hope before I left Trowbridge
and with the Hope the Heart to try any more.   If I
had ever intended to offend, I would be humble
& persevere, but for unintentional offence I have
done enough.   We are not likely to meet often in this
World and if we do, I dare say we shall behave like
reasonable People, who wish each other all that is good
and happy, at least it is so with One of Us.

   " I have seen Mr. Hatchard and he was very communicative respecting ' the strange Gentleman ' who
called on him and I have some Doubt whether our
Friend was not in Earnest when he talked of Writings
and Publications and asked Questions on the latter
Subject: yet it appears strange to us who never, as I
suppose, found him hinting a Wish to enlighten the
World with his Ideas on Matters of so much Importance to us all.   This is between Ourselves for I should
be sorry that he should think me inquisitive after his
purposes, nor indeed was I, Mr Hatchard was desirous
of telling me all that past, and whatever might have
been the Intention at that Time, it is I hope and
believe, laid aside, if not for the best Reason at least
for a prudent One.

   " I am vexed my dear Miss Waldron when I think
that your Mind is troubled and agitated, for so it must
be in some Degree, by Suggestions and Observations
which make their Impression, not on yours only, but on
Every Mind; I do not mean that any such Remarks
as I allude to, can overthrow that has been long
established and is firmly seated in our Hearts & in

our Understanding but they have their effect in clouding over our Spirits, and making us dwell upon Thoughts that are teazing at all times and sometimes painful.

" There are many Questions which we cannot answer, many Doubts which we cannot solve and many Difficulties which no man can remove, but there are a few strong, invincible Truths by which we must abide and may with Confidence: Books written on the Evidences of Religion, often take into their protection too many points which they had better have left to themselves, but the great and essential Articles are surely immoveable and not to be shaken and therefore we should not shake for them as if they were in Danger.

" We are going to be all enlightened, you know, all on the March of Intellect: Now if it were true that real Learning and sound Knowledge would be the Consequence of all this Agitation of Men's Minds Religion would, I am confident be a Gainer, but how it will fare with a multitude of Enquirers, learned enough to raise Doubts and not to solve them, we may reasonably have our Apprehendsions.

" These my dear Miss Waldron are grave and I fear dull and tedious observations, but I write as I feel and I think with vexation and more than vexation of your being troubled by Views and Notions not your own.   We are somewhere, (I do not recollect the place or the very Words) told to this Effect, that if anyone be a Christian he shall know that the Doctrine is of God: but to this it will be answered: ' prove to us that the Doctrine is of God and we will become Christians.'   Now this I would not undertake to do: there is Evidence sufficient I believe for all who will be at the Pains to seek for it, but the Christian certainly sees things in a Light which is not clear to them who say ' prove to us what you assert.'   Belief is not forced upon us, we must seek it and that humbly.

" And now dear Miss Waldron forgive all this: there are some Ministers who preach by their Lives and Conduct, but I have too many Failings as you know, for me to do this, so I try to preach with such Words as I have; but why to you who do believe?   ' Who are a Christian in heart and understanding.' Happily my dear Friend you are, but I want you to be, if possible, unhurt by such suggestions as I have mentioned.   I cannot be more explicit and as I may never again have the pleasure of addressing you, I felt anxious to write on a Subject so interesting.   I have been hurt by such means & now find myself more firm & more able to resist such Attacks and I can but wish her whom I love as I do you, to have equal freedom from them. I trust then that you will excuse, for the Motive's-Sake all I have written, I need not observe that it is to you only.   I hope my Friends are well & that you are all in much Comfort, your Workmen dismissed & your House inside & out just to your Mind.   Believe me My dear Friend

" faithfully and affectionately yours,

" GEO: CRABBE.

" I had nearly forgotten—natural enough you will say—the little Commissions I troubled you with, pray go on and trust me till my Return and be assured that I shall be very glad to find myself in your Debt: there are other poor people I doubt not who need as much as those whom I mentioned and you will really do me Service if you act for me in such Cases: I forgot to mention the Family whom we called on: if what I then gave will be of use pray repeat the Offering for me & if anything of the kind occur I shall take it as a proof of your Confidence in me, when you act for me as I ought to do."

CRABBE TO CECILIA

[THOUGH the following letter is dated three years earlier than the preceding one, I place it out of order because of a circumstance that may or may not be of some interest. Crabbe's youngest sister, Mary, married Mr. Sparkes, a builder of Aldborough, and Cecilia was their daughter. No further explanation of this letter is necessary, but I have in my possession a copy, in Crabbe's manuscript, of the verses beginning

A ring to me Cecilia sends. . . .

This poem has always been entitled, *On Receiving from A Lady a Present of a Ring*, but at the head of my copy Crabbe has written not this, but *Copy of the Verses to Miss W*. Who was Miss W.? And what had she to do with Cecilia? The copy of verses came to me with the letter to Cecilia Sparkes, though that is not evidence.]

" HAMPSTEAD,
" 18 *Oct^r*, 1825.

" MY DEAR CECILIA

" I should have thanked you for your kind letter some Days since, had I been certain of the Day of my Journey, but Circumstances have made that so doubtful that I would not write till I had made up my Mind or rather till my Friends had allowed me to travel & had considered me as One freed from the Care of the Doctor & the Nurse, for both of whom I have had much Occasion. A Gentleman who is going to Chelmsford is gone to Town this morning & means to take for us Places in some Suffolk-Coach, One that goes to Ipswich I prefer for then I am within two Stages of you & may hope to reach Aldborough in the morning of Thursday, that is by one or two oClock; two at farthest, so that if I be not at your House by that Time do not expect me for that Day, & indeed I may say further that in all probability I shall be able to finish my Journey *by twelve oClock,* tho' I dare not precisely fix on that Hour.   & this is the best View which I can at this Time take of my purposes: they do not depend upon myself.

"I am sorry to learn that my Sister is so much indisposed.   I would think the best & try to do so.   It is some Consolation that she is under the Care of Mr King of whom I have heard so much and from Persons who are likely to be Judges.   Give my Love and tell her how soon I hope to see her: Love to Emma for I think she is at Home.

"Pray my dear Niece remember me very kindly to Mr. Sparkes & thank him for his frank and obliging Invitation which I accept with much Satisfaction. Indeed I want to see you all, not forgetting Aldborough itself.

                    "I am dear Cecilia
                        "your affectionate Uncle
                                "GEO CRABBE."

SAMUEL ROGERS PROPOSES PROSPER MERIMÉE FOR THE ATHENÆUM

[SAMUEL Rogers was one of the original members of the Athenæum Club, founded in 1824. The Secretary informs me that Merimée was duly elected to honorary membership, and enjoyed this privilege on more than one occasion when visiting England. In 1835 Rogers was seventy-two.]

                                     " ST. JAMES'S PLACE,
" SIR   "*March* 31, 1835.

     " May I beg the favor of you to lay before the Committee the name of Prosper Merimée as a fit & proper person to invite as an honorary Member of the Athenæum Club during his short residence in this Country ?

                         " Yours very truly
                           " SAMᴸ ROGERS.

     " Author of *Le Théâtre de Clara Gazul, Le Chronique de Charles le Neuf, La Jaquerie*—& several other works."

TWO LETTERS FROM COLERIDGE

I

[No year is given in the date. The letter is to Mrs. Frere, the wife of George Frere, John Hookham Frere's brother. Dr. Bell was Andrew Bell, a celebrated educationist in his time. " Good Dr. Bell is in town. He came from Keswick, all delight with my little Sara, and quite enchanted with Southey " (Letter from S. T. C. to Sir George Beaumont, Dec. 7, 1811). It was Dr. Bell who came to Coleridge one morning " in no small bustle . . . in consequence of a censure passed on the *Remorse* by a man of great talents . . . who was impartial and thought highly of the work as a whole." Dr. Bell would not divulge the critic's name, but the complaint was that there were " many unequal lines in the play." Coleridge afterwards discovered it to be Gifford; but what the offending lines were " *he* (Dr. Bell) would not say, and *I* do not care " (S. T. C. to Southey, Feb. 8, 1813).]

" *Monday,*
" 2 *April.*

" MY DEAR MADAM
" I will not, no unforeseen insuperable obstacle intervening, fail to avail myself of your kind invitation on Friday next, 6 o'clock. I have too many delightful recollections, and too many grateful emotions, con-

nected with your friendly Fireside to need any additional
inducement, tho' if it were not so, it would be a motive
of no ordinary force that I was likely to meet the man
who beyond all competition is entitled to the name
of the greatest Benefactor of the Race of all now living
Individuals—viz. Dr Bell. Make my best respects
to Mr G. Frere and the young Ladies.

Believe me, my dear Madam, sincerely your obliged
Friend

" S. T. Coleridge."

II.

[There is no date on this letter, but the paper is
water-marked 1823. *Aids to Reflection* first appeared
in 1825, and this letter is addressed to Mr. Hessey, of
Taylor and Hessey who published the book. Coleridge's suggestions as to arrangement were adopted by
the printers.]

" Dear Sir
" You will see by the accompanying that I
have been busily and anxiously employed since I last
saw you. As soon as I saw the Proof, I was struck
with the apprehension of the disorderly and hetero-
geneous appearance which the Selections intermixed
with my own comments etc would have—I had not
calculated aright on the relative quantity of the one
and the other. And the more I reflected, the more
desirable it appeared to me to carry on the promise
of the Title Page (*Aids* to reflection) systematically
throughout the work. But little did I anticipate the
time and trouble, that this *refacciamento* would cost

me. Mrs Gillman could inform you, that with the exception of a few days of Illness I have been at work on this Volume & the Essay on the times of Leighton & the causes of the Schism in Protestantism, every day of my absence, from Breakfast to Dinner and from Tea to Bed time—merely allowing myself two hours for Bathing and Exercise.

"On the return of the next proofs, the conclusion of the last Division (Spiritual and Philosophical) will accompany them. And the historical & biographical essay shall be ready. I suspect it will stand in strange *contrast* of Opinion with Southey's *Church*, which will come out about the same time!

"I leave it to your better judgement; but it strikes me that by printing the Aphorisms *numerically* with interspace, as I have written them—thus—

Aphorism I.

Then the title or heading of it, if any: and then the passage itself, would be so very much the best way, as to make it worth while—And instead of the (Leighton, Vol. 8, p. —) at the *end*, simply to have an L. either thus

Aphorism V. L.

or before the first word of the Aphorism, on the same line with it.

L.   A reflecting mind, etc—

and when it is not Leighton's, to put either E. (Editor's) or nothing.

"In those Aphorisms, in which part only is Leighton's, they might be marked L. E.

" But I shall call on you, please God, on Tuesday Morning.

" Your obliged
" S. T. COLERIDGE.

" If it were feared that there is too much matter, all the extracts from 1, 2 of p. 52, viz. Aphorisms, 12, 13, 14, 15, might be omitted.

" MR. HESSEY."

BLOOMFIELD AND BURNS

[ROBERT BLOOMFIELD (1766-1823), like Shenstone, has always been a name; but, unlike Shenstone, he has little virtue left in his poetry when we turn to it again. But he had the good fortune to find Bewick as an illustrator, and his books at least are worth the small change for which they can be bought. Not much of a poet, and yet the cobbler was something of a story, and no one would grudge him the wisp of fame that is still his.

The following letter, the original of which is in my possession, cannot be strictly said to be unpublished, but I think that it may properly be included in the present collection. The circumstances were these.

The letter was written to David Steuart Erskine (1742-1829), eleventh Earl of Buchan, and brother of Henry Erskine the Lord Advocate. Buchan was an enthusiastic, though it seems somewhat eccentric, patron of arts and letters, and Bloomfield was one of his protégés. The following extract from a letter written by Lord Buchan to Longman and Company explains the circumstances in which Bloomfield's letter was written:

" I was, while in the Adelphi, to sit for my portrait to the Rev. William Gardiner, then become bookseller in union with Mr Harding, engraver, etc., in Pall Mall, and having made a sentimental visit to the birth-place of Newton, at Woolsthorp, I was to be represented venerating the spot and the orchard where that great

257

man first conceived, by the falling of an apple, the theory of gravitation, in its application to the motions of the heavenly bodies. While I sat for my picture I happened to mention the sudden and extraordinary manner of my mother's death, accompanied with circumstances preceding it, which are of too sacred and too private a nature to be revealed at present.

" I invited him down to Scotland that I might have him at Dryburgh Abbey, and show him the pastoral scenes that adjoin it, the pure parent stream of Eden, & of Tweed, where Thomson first tuned his pastoral pipe, and I asked him to come to the Adelphi next day, to honour my sitting for the painting of my portrait. Prevented by a headache, he could not come, but sent me an apology hastily written, of which the following is a copy, and which being, as he frankly says in it, a picture of his own mind, I have thought it a proper introduction to his ' Wild Flowers,' and recommend it accordingly to the readers of that little volume.

" BUCHAN.

" MESSRS. LONGMAN & CO.,
  " BOOKSELLERS,
    " PATERNOSTER ROW, LONDON."

Lord Buchan's letter itself, from which the above extract is taken, was written in 1806, when Longman (plus the usual bevy of names) published Bloomfield's *Wild Flowers*. Lord Buchan enclosed a copy of the letter from Bloomfield here printed, and proposed that this, together with his own letter, should be prefixed to future editions of that book. This communication was forwarded by Rees (one of the bevy) to the poet, asking whether he wished Lord Buchan's suggestion to be adopted. Bloomfield then submitted the matter to his friend and patron Capel Lofft, who had sponsored the first publication of *The Farmer's Boy* in 1800. As is the way with patrons, Lofft could sometimes be a tiresome person, and on this occasion he wrote a heavy letter to Bloomfield, advising him to do nothing to hurt Lord Buchan's sensibilities. So far as I can discover, however, the letters were not included in any edition of *Wild Flowers*. The manuscripts relating to the matter, including two copies of Bloomfield's letter, are among the Bloomfield manuscripts in the British Museum, and W. H. Hart in his *Selections from the Correspondence of Robert Bloomfield* made in 1870 prints Bloomfield's letter. As, however, the pamphlet is itself hard to find, I like to use my manuscript for the purpose of printing the letter here.

With all its imperfections of style and taste the letter makes its appeal, and the passage about Burns is rather a gallant one. Bloomfield's allusion to the Preface to *Rural Tales* (1802) refers to the following:

"I have received many honourable testimonies of esteem from strangers; letters without a name, but fill'd with the most cordial advice, and almost a parental anxiety, for my safety under so great a share of public applause. I beg to refer such friends to the great teacher Time: and hope that he will hereafter give me my deserts, and no more."]

"My Lord,   "*Jany* 19th, 1802.
    "It may look strange that one who has repeatedly been honoured with your Lordship's conversation should have anything left to express by writing. But

the sudden transition from shade to sunshine, from obscurity to publicity which have fallen to my lot has sometimes proved almost painful, and often perplexing to a great degree.

" Condescension from superiors ought at least to inspire confidence sufficient to meet their approbation in all its shapes and modifications; and when it do not, I am apt to suspect that it deserves no such plausible name as Modesty; it is a dastardly child the Ofspring of Ignorance and Fear. I feel, and know, that in my composition there is not an attom of what is call'd Wit. My reply's are the slow suggestions of contemplation and my ' good things ' mostly come half an hour too late. I find this to be true in conversations with my equals, where restraint can have no force. There is however another enemy, (though in some cases my dearest friend) whose power is resistless, and whose visits are perpetually made known by a rising of the stomach and a redundancy of water in the eyes. Subjects of interest to the feelings are frequent in parties such as I have lately had the honour to join; where, independent of the subject being often above my reach, I find this weakness, if it be a weakness, stand in my way and absolutely obstruct any remark or reply whatever. Your Lordship informed me particularly of the Death of a Lady, the circumstances attending which were of a singular and uncommonly interesting nature. I know not whither to wish such scenes to fall in my way, or whither to rejoice selfishly that I have no such torture, for excess of pleasure certainly becomes pain. I have never frequented so desirable and honourable a school as that in which your Lordship presides; I mean your friendly conversations with the learned and the good, the very Cream of a Nation's talents; and when I reflect on what I am,

I can but wonder at that one qualification which alone is thought sufficient to entitle me to be amongst you. The clashing of animated Spirits, the Flint and Steel of conversation; though it communicates no fire, gives me a glorious light; and while, I suppress my own thoughts I often hear them better advanced, and better cloath'd by another.

"The illustrious Soul that has left amongst us the name of Burns, has often been lower'd down to a comparison with me, but the comparison exists more in circumstances than in essentials. That man stood up with the stamp of superior intellect on his brow, a visible greatness: and great and patriotic subjects would only have called into action the powers of his mind, which lay inactive while he play'd calmly and exquisitely the Pastoral Pipe. The Letters to which I have alluded in my Preface to the 'Rural Tales,' were friendly warnings, pointed with immediate reference to the fate of that extraordinary man. 'Remember Burns,' has been the watchword of my friends. I do remember Burns, but I *am not* Burns! neither have I his fire to fan nor to quench; nor his passions to controul! Where then is my merit if I make a peaceful voyage on a smooth Sea, and with no Mutiny on board? To a Lady, (I have it from herself) who remonstrated with him on his danger from drink, and the persuits of some of his associates, he reply'd— 'Madam they would not thank me for my company if I did not drink with them, I *must* give them a slice of my constitution.' How much to be regretted that he did not give them thinner slices of his constitution that it might have lasted longer!

"I write this my Lord under the twinges of a Headach to which I am subject, and which has prevented my waiting on your Lordship this morning. If in my

fireside recollections I thus draw a picture of myself,
I hope I do not trespass on Mr. Gardner's profession;
and more particularly I hope I shall not trespass on
your Lordship's patience. I feel so great a triumph
in having your decided approbation that I cannot for-
bear hazarding an avowal of it in writing. I have said

"¡Nature's sublimer scenes ne'er charm'd mine eyes,"

and what effect the Cambrian or Caledonian Mountains,
or a sight of the Sea would have, I can only guess.
These to me, are distant visionary raptures, like the
Saint's prospects of Heaven. My 'Emma's Kid'
is therefore the dream of imagination; and the eye
has no share in collecting any one Idea to identify
the picture.

" If a Man is set upon a House-top, he must be a fool
not to tread with caution, and feel a becoming solicitude for his safety; more particularly so, if, amongst the
spectators some might be found who would like to see
him fall. This is my situation in some degree. The
patronage of Wealth and conspicuous talents may well
be envied, and perhaps will as long as envy dwells in
little souls, and true Nobility in great ones. Though
I know that I am incomprehensible to myself, and thus
call my courage and confidence to a reconing for sailors
I know that a small dose of poison, alias Spirits, has
a momentary influence in strengthening both. But,
My Lord, as I have a strong predeliction for living as
long as I can, and for living with your Lordship's favour
upon my head, I beseech you at all times, and on all
occasions to guard your decisions with your accustom'd
sence and candor, and never to believe that Bloomfield
is turn't fool untill you see it yourself.

" Indeed I much question the wisdom of my counteracting and opposing my watry-headed propensity at all. The indulgence of it is more precious than the wealth of all the Distiliries in the World; and I have allways written best when I have indulged it most.—But I perceive that I am tattling like Old Richard all about myself, and beg pardon for thus troubling your Lordship with the fruits of the Headach, and the stirrings of Gratitude, and perhaps of ambition; but I will never be ashamed of any of them while I hold Life, and your Lordship's good opinion.

" ROBT. BLOOMFIELD.

"*Jan. 19th*, 1802."

[The Hart collection prints another letter from Bloomfield to Lord Buchan, dated February 16, 1802, in which we find—" Your Lordship's invitation to the shades of Dryburgh is noble. I have ardent wishes on that point, and have some reasons which rise up against their completion, two of which are—Burns is dead, or I might have seen him—I am married."]

JOHN CLARE IN 1830

[BLOOMFIELD's name, if not altogether forgotten, survives at best in very faded characters, while John Clare's reputation, always in good keeping, now shines with a fixed brightness in English poetry, lovingly tended as it has recently been by Mr. Arthur Symons and Mr. Edmund Blunden. It is pleasant to remember that in his time Clare, with more generosity than truth it may be allowed, wrote a sonnet

TO THE MEMORY OF BLOOMFIELD.*

Sweet unassuming Minstrel! not to thee
   The dazzling fashions of the day belong;
Nature's wild pictures, field, and cloud, and tree,
   And quiet brooks, far distant from the throng,
In murmurs tender as the toiling bee,
   Make the sweet music of thy gentle song.
Well! Nature owns thee: let the crowd pass by;
   The tide of fashion is a stream too strong
For pastoral brooks, that gently flow and sing:
   But Nature is their source, and earth and sky
Their annual offering to her current bring.
   Thy gentle muse and memory need no sigh;
For thine shall murmur on to many a spring,
   When prouder streams are summer-burnt and dry.

The following letter to his publisher, John Taylor, formerly of Taylor and Hessey, and now in business alone, was written by Clare in 1830. This, according

* *The Rural Muse*, 1835, p. 127.

to Frederick Martin, Clare's first biographer, and
Mr. Blunden, was the serenest period of the poet's life.
"He almost wondered," says Martin, "why he had
ever despaired—happiness, after all, seemed so cheap
and within such easy reach"; and Mr. Blunden:
"This salutary state of affairs lasted through 1830,
until happiness seemed the only possibility before him."
He was in work, he was getting some money from
publishers and editors, and he was happy with his
family.   Though the family was formidable; this
letter is dated October 2, and Martin records,
"Patty presented him with another baby—sixth
in the list; baptized Sophia, on the 3rd of October,
1830."

This unpublished letter, however, indicates the
pathetic standards by which Clare's serenity has to be
measured.   If this be content, the misfortunes of his
life were bitter indeed, and the asylum days that were
to come might well be his first discovery of peace.
Clare was in the habit of getting copies of his book
The Shepherd's Calendar (1827) at cost price and selling
them locally for what few pence of profit he could get.
The letter was no doubt occasioned by some such
transaction.   Like Bloomfield, Clare was lucky in his
illustrator, or notably in one of them.   The 1827
volume contains a lovely frontispiece from a drawing
by Peter De Wint, whom Clare knew, and to whom
he refers in the letter.   And he wrote a better sonnet
than the one to Bloomfield.

To De Wint*

Dewint! I would not flatter; nor would I
   Pretend to critic-skill in this thy art;
Yet in thy landscapes I can well descry
   The breathing hues as Nature's counterpart.
No painted peaks, no wild romantic sky,
   No rocks, nor mountains, as the rich sublime,
Hath made thee famous; but the sunny truth
   Of Nature, that doth mark thee for all time,
Found on our level pastures:—spots, forsooth,
   Where common skill sees nothing deemed divine.
Yet here a worshipper was found in thee;
   And thy young pencil worked such rich surprise.
That rushy flats, befringed with willow tree,
   Rivalled the beauties of Italian skies.   ]

                                        " Helston.
" My dear Taylor   " Oct. 2, 1830.
      " I am very disappointed in not receiving an
answer to my last letter because I wrote it under
much difficulty when I was scarcely able to manage
the pen as I wanted some copies of the Poems down as
quick as possible & I expected to see them long ago
but I fancy you was not at home when it arrived &
therefore I have written again & hope you will reply
as soon as you can—I have been dreadfully unwell &
I am sorry to say that I often feel apprehensions of
a return of the illness that distresses me very much
by times tho I do all I can to keep up my spirits—I
again repeat the desire that I expressed in my last
letter that you will have the kindness to send the books
as soon as you can—I have no other news to write
about & as to my road at this present in the wilderness
it is all barren.   Still I am yours sincerely
                                        " John Clare.

         * The Rural Muse, p. 133.

" Have you seen Dewint if not have the kindness to remind him ere you send off the books & let me hear from you by letter that you receive this & when I may expect the parcel as I will send over to Deeping for it

" Yours J. C."

FROM LETTERS FROM GEORGE DARLEY (1795-1846) TO ALLAN CUNNINGHAM (1784-1842)

[MR. C. C. ABBOTT, of King's College, Aberdeen, is at present engaged on a much needed Life and Letters of Darley. If my inferences as to the circumstances of the following letters, all of which are undated, are in some points wrong, I hope he will be able to correct me.

It may be noted that in his *History of British Literature*, 1834, Cunningham says of Darley, he "is a true poet and excellent mathematician. There is much compact and graceful poetry in his *May Queen* [Sylvia]; and in *The Olympian Revels* a dramatic freedom and fervour too seldom seen in song."

I.

The *London Magazine* for August, 1821, has "the pleasure to introduce to its readers the first of a series of valuable papers in continuation of Dr. Johnson's *Lives of the English Poets* . . . etc." Cunningham was by now an important contributor to that magazine, and Darley was to become one two years later. The following letter was doubtless written in this connection, and the day, July 14, is probably of the year 1821.

Of Cunningham's relations with Southey a glimpse is given in a letter that follows these from Darley.]

" 14 *July.*

" My dear Friend,

"I have looked over your List of Poets, and even had I all my recollections about me, could scarce add another good name to the number. It would perhaps be cruel to congratulate you on knowing so many. Full one half of them, we should both agree, are less fit for Olympus than the Paradise of Fools. But being compelled to keep square with Johnson, I acknowledge you can scarcely get rid of them. This is the fruit of having to cater for the public swallow. When Leviathan is to be fed, we must leave in bushels of garbage, or the great bathos of his stomach would never feel itself filled. Had we to make our own List, it would be far different. No ingenuity can erect a noble structure on the base of Johnson. Taking so low a standard, do what you will the work, if carried out, would be less like the Lives of the Poets than the Lives of All who have ever writ Verses. What of good may be done on such a plan, I know no one more capable of effecting than yourself, but it is not an employment I fear much more congenial to your tastes than my own.

" You conceive yourself no doubt obliged to exclude from your List all who have never written any but dramatic Poetry. Else wherefore omit such names as Marston, Middleton, Heywood, Decker, Webster, & others ? For my own part I do not see why certain scores of the Ducks and Dukes should not give place to our Early Dramatists, and so furnish out indeed a complete as well as unblotted Scroll of British Poets. Johnson's Lives should remain, as the Devil's harangues in Milton, tho' made up of spite, slander, wrong-headedness, bluster, & blasphemy. But they should remain for their abstract merit as glowing ebullitions

of the brain, not for what pismire Malone calls them,
' the finest body of criticism in the world.'

" On second thoughts, and finding in what a truck-
way you must run, do not let me be anywise influential
about making you re-write Milton's life, unless you
find it advisable yourself. But by all means, and as
you would have the Serpent at the root of your own
laurel destroyed, render Johnson innocuous in your
notes on the worst piece of posthumous assassination.
I coincide with you against Southey as to the Dates.

" Your sincere wellwisher

" GEORGE DARLEY.

"Here follows a set of names, some of which may
not be in your List yet deserve it as well as some that are:

> Chamberlayne—author of Pharronida.
> Giles Fletcher.
> Merrick.
> G. Herbert.
> I. Chalkhill—*vide* Iz. Walton.
> Moore—the fabulist.
> Matthew Green—author of the ' Spleen.'
> C. Cotton.
> Smart.
> Ogilvie.
> Shaw.
> Sir R. Maithland.
> Robertson—' Argentine.'

" ALLAN CUNNINGHAM, ESQ."

II.

[The date of this letter was probably 1827 or 1828.
Scott's *Napoleon* appeared in the latter part of 1827,
and by then Cunningham was busy with the prepara-

tion of the *Anniversary* for 1829, of which he had undertaken the editorship. Darley was a contributor.

" Ferintosh " I take to be a beverage; but of what nature I am ignorant beyond the hint that Darley gives.

Charles Lamb had, Mr. Lucas tells us, invited Cunningham " to an evening party of *London Magazine* contributors " in 1821. In 1825 Lamb writes of the *London*: " Our 2nd No. is all trash. . . . The only clever hand they have is Darley. . . ." And in 1826 he asks H. F. Cory to " gladden our cell by accompanying our old chums of the *London*, Darley and Allan Cunningham, to Enfield on Wednesday." He adds that Darley knows all about the coaches. In this connection I should like to boast that I have a copy of the first edition of *Sylvia* (1827), given by Darley to Lamb's Miss Kelly.

Of his stammering Darley himself spoke as " a hideous mask upon his mind, which not only disfigures but nearly suffocates it."]

" My dear Allan   " *Wednesday.*
        " Many thanks for the Ferintosh—if it be as honest (in its way) as the Sender I shall be satisfied with it, tho' I am not much of an Irishman as to adoration of ishkabaugh. You must come some night and give it a higher relish by your conversation.
        " I saw C. Lamb—spent a delightful two days with him—could hardly get away, & have promised to go there soon again—without a formal invitation, which he hates. He is so devilish idle that I fear for *all* to

whom he has promised contributions. I am however to see the MS. of a play he has lately written—and I was just thinking whether ' A Scene from an Unpublished Play' by C. Lamb, might not be suitable to you. Should you like this ?—if so I will endeavor to procure it.

"Of course I should very much like to see Southey, as a man whose learning & genius I estimate highly— But do not think of asking him on *my account*—I should only gape & stare at him, as I did at Wordsworth & Coleridge t'other night—Or perhaps make a fool of myself if I attempted to stammer out an observation.

"You are getting on rapidly I hear with the Annual —and I hope satisfactorily too.

"Yours most truly

"A. Cunningham, Esq. "G. D.

"My good fellow, I must make a clear *demand* of you for a loan of Scott's Napoleon—it is but this moment I have heard you possess a copy, or you should not have read it in peace for my importunity."

III.

[This letter, which has no signature, but is complete with its postscript, belongs, I think, to 1834, when Gainsborough's " Blue Boy " and " Cottage Door " were exhibited together at the British Institution, as we learn from Mr. Maurice Brockwell's handsome catalogue of Mr. Henry E. Huntingdon's collection, into which both pictures are now gathered in California.

Darley was for some years art critic for the *Athenæum*, but what the intention of this communication

to Cunningham may have been I do not know.   The
London Magazine days were over.]

" MY DEAR ALLAN   " *Friday Eve.*
   " Just returned from the Grosvenor Gallery.
I did not, like a farthing-faced personage whom I saw
there, ' take notes on the spot,' either by way of displaying my purple-leather pocketbook, or of making
believe that I was profoundly immersed in critical
reflection.   But the engravings of almost all those noble
paintings are yet sharp enough in my brain to furnish
you with clear impressions—tho' I cannot answer for
their correctness, as the tablet was not very well
prepared for what it was to receive.   With respect to
the Gainsboroughs, of which you especially desire an
unsophisticated Critic's opinion (just to see, I imagine,
what a ninny poor Nature is, without her governess *Art*
to tell her what she should say on every occasion): with
respect to the Gainsboroughs, I had as little difficulty
in forming a judgment, right or wrong, as I have much
in forming any judgment *at all* with respect to many
works of more celebrated Artists.   For example one of
the Titians in this Collection appears to me like a huge
square *palette* of mingled colours: I can make nothing
of it: whether it be worthy the inside of a palace or the
outside of an alehouse, I have not the most remote
idea: perhaps of both, the colors of one, and the
composition of the other.   But as to the Blue Boy,
and the Cottage Door,—these do not give one the
trouble of *growing* an opinion, it shoots up at once
spontaneously.   On entering the Salon, your eye is
immediately caught over your left shoulder by rather
a singular object.   If you will abide by a canon established by one who has formed a sort of creed in the

Fine Arts for himself,—any painting which, at first sight, strikes, without striking by an obvious excellence, is in some particular or other *faulty*. There must be something *outré*, or eccentric, in it, which takes the attention, not the admiration, prisoner by surprise or stratagem: and everything of this violent nature is a harshness to the taste and feelings. In this principle I am borne out, to my own sensation, by the Blue Boy. Its singularity of costume—being a youthful figure clad in silvery-azure satin from top to toe, as I have seen a stuffed puppet,—strikes, yet does not immediately gratify. One exclaims—how *odd !* how fantastic ! Which is the same thing, perhaps, as saying—this rather offends me ! But then you reflect—have I never seen a *real* Blue Boy; in other words,—have I never seen a little boy in blue coat and trousers, whom yet I thought (or at least, who might be) a very gallant, noble little fellow ?—Yes; but undoubtedly you would rather have seen him less singularly apparelled. In Gainsborough's time there were, probably, several children of noblemen so dressed on gala-days: but many upon seeing them no doubt observed that their dress was not tasteful, some that it was positively ill-chosen, and to the eye of a painter or a person of delicate taste in colors, it must have been disagreeable and even offensive. In like manner, I would say that Gainsborough's Blue Boy was, so far as regards this point, faulty: it rather offends a commonly-educated eye, and would perhaps violently offend one that was highly cultivated. If such be the case, it decides the question between Gainsborough and Reynolds in favor of the latter: not however if he affirmed the impossibility of executing an *agreeable* picture wherein *blue* was the prominent color, but only if he affirmed the impossibility of executing a picture of this sort which should *not offend* by that prominent color. The Blue Boy certainly does offend by its cerulean uniformity of appearance, at first sight; tho' its merits, in *other* respects, render it on the whole an agreeable picture,—indeed so agreeable as to efface, in a short time, almost every recollection that it had once offended you. The figure stands easily and firmly, as if every square-inch of the soles of *both* feet touched and felt the earth under them: which to me has something very *satisfactory* in it. I am afraid of the object slipping down the canvas, as *should* frequently happen in paintings where you see figures sitting on the edge of a chair, or standing where a goat could not support itself a moment. The Blue Boy is a portrait I believe of the Artist's own son: yet there is a princely character in his attitude,—the grandeur of *mind*, we are to suppose, ennobling him—giving the impression of a Royal Highness the Duke of York or of Gloucester in court dress one or two centuries ago. A tender softness or mellowness of hue into which this cerulean monotony which we blame at first is reduced,—nay a degree of warmth by no means to be expected,—form perhaps the most remarkable quality we observe in the painting. It appears to me that the Artist caught this lovely tint from a view of the horizontal sky, or calm surface of the distant ocean, a little after sunrise, of a breathless summer's morning: both have that smooth silver-blue tint and warmth of tone which distinguish the drapery of the portrait, azure tho' it be to the very fullblown ribbands on the instep and the point of the shoe itself. As to the countenance, tho' I cannot say whether it was ever like any living being, it is certainly very like life. What a countenance can exhibit beyond fidelity and reality, is I believe *sentiment* and nothing more,—I mean something

characteristic, favourable or unfavourable. There is
a great deal of this in Gainsborough's portrait; it does
not merely look straight before it as if a sail were in
view, nor follow you all round the room with its
white *sights* till you wish it turned to the wall, like
those innumerable glaring physiognomies at Somerset
House which make your eyes ake to look at them. It is
the countenance of an ingenuous & intelligent boy,
with the air of immediate thought in every feature.
The background of the picture is smoky and confused,
but detaches the figure very well from the canvas; and
this is all for which it was requisite. Take it for all in all,
I can only say that I wish our future Artists may be
at any time entitled to despise the Blue Boy: for in that
case they must far excel Velasquez and Vandyke, nay
Titian himself.

"Nearly opposite the Blue Boy is Gainsborough's
other famous work—the Cottage Door. This repre-
sents a Cottage Matron with an infant in her arms,
and several other children around her 'supping *broo*'
at the door of a cabin. The whole is a buried scene,
deeply shut up in a close, wooded nook. There is
great breadth and mass about it; with a richness of
coloring, or a *brown goldenness*, .which I think generally
distinguishes the landscapes of this Artist. He reminds
me more of Gaspar Poussin, tho' not in this quality,
than any ancient master I can think of at present:
there is the same deepness of background, and inflexi-
bility of foliage, about both. Indeed, I can hardly
feel myself *amongst* the trees of any landscape-painter
but Claude; there is such wonderful ease and freedom
of attitude about them! they are the only painted
trees which seem to *blow*. G. Poussin's, on the contrary, are such wooden trees! His foliage consists,
as it were, of *heaps of hands* with spread fingers—the

leaves all diverge like trefoil, quatrefoil, etc. I recognize the same fault, or an approach to it, in almost all landscapes but those of Claude; and by this test alone I would decide upon the Marriage of Rebecca at the National Gallery being genuine—tho' defective in some points, the foliage determines it a Claude at once; no one but he could have given it that *roundness*, and miniature delicacy, airiness, and mobility. Gainsborough's foliage in the above painting strikes me as coarse, blotchy, and stiff. But the largeness of manner, and depth of body, which this landscape, as well as all of his I have ever seen, presents, are with me great recommendations. Not to speak of the beautiful group, (in which by the by we see the *pyramid-law* perhaps too geometrically observed); and their manifest state of living existency! The Matron herself is, perhaps, the most natural beau-ideal of a youthful Cottage Dame, on canvas: rustic beauty exalted by a gentility of expression which we seldom find in the peasant countenance, if ever.

"Thus you have nearly all I felt and thought on the Gainsborough aforesaid—there was I believe a third, but as I had not much time to spare, being rather late, I did not look at it. Probably the greatest error in this homebred critique is its originality—I should have imbibed a taste, not instituted one of my own. But you know I am of the small sect of Independents with regard to Literature, and Arts—indeed everything.

" *P.S.*—When I begun this sketch I had intended copying it out, if worth the trouble, from the blotting-paper on which it is written—but as it is legible enough I send it without being transcribed, especially as I do not know that I could much improve it by any pains in alteration. Such as it is make whatever use of it you please.

" ALLAN CUNNINGHAM, ESQ.
 " 27 LOWER BELGRAVE PLACE."

IV.

[The date of this must be between 1839, when Darley's *Nepenthe* was privately printed, and 1842, when Cunningham died. The eight volumes were probably the latter's edition of Burns, with a *Life*, which appeared in that form in 1834.]

" MY DEAR ALLAN   " 29 *June*.
 " As a poor return for your eight splendid Volumes, will you accept my sorry little pamphlet of a Poem ? One half finished work out of an hundred which indolence & hopelessness united keep me from concluding. I was pretty sure no Publisher would undertake it in any shape, and therefore printed a few copies of this part myself for the small number of friends who care about my verses. The greatest recommendation I can give you of my Nepenthe is that it fulfils Mrs. Cunningham's wish about Sylvia, being ' all prologue.'

      " Yours in weal & woe
       " GEORGE DARLEY.

 " The second copy is for your Son, if he also will do me the favor to accept.

" ALLAN CUNNINGHAM, ESQ."

ALLAN CUNNINGHAM TO ROBERT SOUTHEY

[The "two little volumes" were the *Traditional Tales of the English and Scottish Peasantry*, published in 1822. Cunningham's trade had first been that of a mason. Then, drifting into authorship in the meantime, he became assistant to "Mr. Bubb, an inferior sculptor," whom he offended by transferring his services to the great Chantrey. Then he became a man of letters wholly. The dramatic story of which a second edition was called for was presumably *Sir Marmaduke Maxwell*, published in March, 1822.]

"Eccleston Street,
"Pimlico.
"*July 22nd,* 1822.
"Dear Sir,
        "In the two little volumes of north country stories of which I request your acceptance it has been my wish to revive something like the old popular desultory way of tale telling once very prevalent among the peasantry. I have interspersed them with songs and ballads for those oral stories had their rhymes also. They are founded generally in traditions with which I became acquainted on the two shores of Solway.
        "I have to thank you for a very kind and gratifying letter which has been perused right frequently. I

shall keep it to cheer me when fits of doubting and despondency come. I am far from liable to be gloomy yet there are times when I glance back to earlier days almost tempted to cry aloud with Burns ' Had I to gude advice but harkit.' The place which a love of poesie has filled in my heart might have been supplied by some more profitable thing, but I was bred in a lonely place, painting and sculpture seemed something like the work of sorcery and unattainable and as my trade presented nothing to please my ambition I was fain in my twenty-first year to wooe the more accessible muse of homely country rhymes.

"You will be pleased to hear that a second edition of my dramatic story is called for, I have endeavoured to profit by the remarks of some kind friends in making amendments. But it is only in trifles that a story can be mended—once wrong and ever wrong—at least the proverb holds good with me. I wish to try another native story, and when once I have made a rough sketch or model I shall endeavour to acquit myself as well as I may—probably something like a dramatic romance in blank verse interspersed with lyrics would be more in my way than anything else.

"I am not sure that I shall pass to Solway before next year—but Keswick shall lie in my way were it at the other side of the island. I have some hopes however of seeing you in London before I go to the north—a Bust of the author of Roderick the last of the Goths is much wanted from the hand of Mr Chantrey. I have got an engraving by Reynolds from the painting of Mr Phillips which recalls you very strongly to my mind—that of Crabbe is also excellent, in Sir Walter Scott I think him less happy and Campbell is a failure.

One of Chantrey's Busts is a portrait all round and therefore superior to painting.

"I have the honour to subscribe myself
"Your sincere admirer & faithful friend
"ALLAN CUNNINGHAM.

"To ROBERT SOUTHEY, Esq."

INDEX

ARNOLD, MATTHEW, 20, 22
death of his sons, 224, 225
his and Browning's *Glanvil*, 216,
217
relations with Browning, 216,
217, 218, 226-232
Ashley Library catalogue, 191, 192,
200
Pope first editions, 192, 193,
194
Prior first editions, 194
Rossetti first editions, 194, 195

Barnes, W., an Admirable Crichton,
182
a dandy, 182
and Dorset dialect, 182, 183
first poems, 184
and Thomas Hardy, 183, 185
last poem, 186
monument, 181
unpublished letters, 186-188
Beattie, J., and Mrs. Montagu, 243
portrait, 242
unpublished letter, 243, 244
Bloomfield, R., and Clare, 264
details of early publications, 258,
259
estimate of Burns, 261
letter from Lord Buchan, 257
letter to Lord Buchan, 259-263
Book-binding, 195, 196
Book collecting, 191, 207
Brontë, Charlotte, 46, 47, 48, 50, 52
Emily, 47, 50, 53
Anne, 48, 50
Brontë, P. B., A. C. Benson's edition,
45, 46
Caractacus MS., 46
Mrs. Gaskell and, 44, 46, 51, 53
Leyland's Life of, 44, 48, 52, 53

Brontë, P. B., as painter, 45, 46, 51, 54
poetry, 44, 45, 49, 53, 54
translating Horace, 54, 57, 58
Browning, R. See Arnold, M.
Burns, 20, 261

Clare, John, and Bloomfield, 264
his circumstances, 265
and De Wint, 265, 266, 267
unpublished letter, 266, 267
Coleridge, D., 158, 159, 162, 164
Coleridge, H., 54
birth and death, 157
childhood, 159
critical judgment, 162
early improvisations, 160
estimate of, 162, 163
gains Oxford Scholarship and
Fellowship, 160; and loses it,
161
habit of annotation, 161, 162
intemperance, 158, 161
in Lake District, 159, 161
portraits of, 157
unpublished letters, 163-165
and Wordsworth, 159, 161
Coleridge, S. T., 157, 158, 159, 161,
162, 165, 253, 272
Aids to Reflection, 254, 255
bibliography of, 95 *n.*
and the Gillmans, 63-69, 255
his copy of *Milton*:
its pedigree, 69
his annotations, 70-91
takes opium, 63, 64
unpublished letters, 253-256
Zapolya:
first published, 95
emendations, 97-99
Collop, John, best poems, 121 *et seq.*
" discovery of," 117

283

Cory, W., as country squire, 8, 15-17
  as Eton master, 4, 8, 13, 14, 15
  and Drummond, 38
  family name, 3
  great men his pupils, 13
  Heraclitus, 6
  heretical literary opinions, 20
    et seq.
  Hints for Eton Masters, 13 *n.*
  his son, 18
  Ionica, 3, 11, 19
  Letters and Journals, 9, 10, 11,
    13, 38
  Lord Esher's *Ionicus*, 12, 13, 19
  marriage, 18
  and music, 27, 28
  near-sighted, 14
  as patriot, 12
  philosophy of life, 24
  Reparabo, 5
  as talker, 10
  titles of best poems, 4
  unpublished letters, 29-37
  unpublished poem, 38, 39

Darley, G., art critic, 272-277
  estimate of Johnson, 269, 270
  and Lamb, 271, 272
Darwin, E., birth and death, 143
  Botanic Garden, 144 *et seq.*, 153
    Canning's Parody, 147
  and Cowper, 143, 148
  doubtful science of, 149
  Economy of Vegetation, 151, 152
  Loves of the Plants, 144, 150
  meets Johnson, 143
  and Miss Seward, 144, 145
  Temple of Nature, 148, 151, 152

Esher, Lord, Cory's pupil, 12, 13
  his *Ionicus*, 19

Gainsborough's *Blue Boy*, 273-276
Gaskell, Mrs., 44, 46, 51, 53
Gosse, Sir E., 192
  his library, 200
    some rarities in, 201
  E. H. M. Cox's catalogue of,
    199 *n.*, 202
  literary estimate of, 199

Gosse, Sir E., tragic note on Omar,
  203

Hardy, T., 175, 181, 183, 185,
  201
Hawker, R. S., eccentric habits and
    dress, 170, 174, 175
  and Godwin, 175
  and Hardy, 175
  life, 169 *et seq.*
  loved by the poor, 171, 172
  parish magazine, 176
  poetry, 176, 177, 178
  twice married, 174
  unpublished poem, 178
Horace, 54, 55, 56, 57, 58

Johnson, Dr., 143, 242, 268, 269

Keats, letters, 215

Lamb, Charles, 163, 271, 272
Landor, W. S., characteristic con-
    fusion of MS., 103, 104, 108
  Dry Sticks Fagoted:
    first published, 103
    unpublished letters refer-
      ring to, 103-114

Milton, 69-91, 109, 119, 134

Seatonian Prize, 137, 138
Shakespeare, 21
Shenstone, W., 257
  letters, 237
  life, 236-238
  unpublished letter, 239-241
Smart, Christopher, and Seatonian
    Prize, 137, 138
  uncollected poem, 138, 139
Southey, 160, 268, 272, 279-281

Tennyson, 20, 22, 25, 28

Wise, T. J., bibliographies, 95 *n.*,
  110
  his library. See Ashley Library
Wordsworth, 20, 21, 50, 159, 161,
  272